# SPIRITUAL DIALECTICS

By

SWAMI MUKUNDANANDA

Published by:
**Jagadguru Kripaluji Yog**
7405, Stoney Point Dr
Plano, TX 75025
USA

www.jkyog.org

ISBN: 978-0-9826675-9-0

# About the Author

Swami Mukundananda is a world-renowned spiritual teacher from India, and is the senior disciple of Jagadguru Shree Kripaluji Maharaj. He is the founder of the Yogic system called "Jagadguru Kripaluji Yog."

Swamiji is a unique *sanyāsī* (in the renounced order of life), who has a distinguished technical and management educational background as well. He completed B.Tech. from the world-renowned Indian Institute of Technology (IIT), Delhi. He then did MBA from the equally distinguished Indian Institute of Management (IIM), Kolkata. After that, he worked for some time with one of India's topmost industrial houses.

However, distinguished material education and a promising corporate career did not quench his thirst for knowing the Absolute Truth. The longing for God was so strong that he renounced his career and traveled throughout India as a *sanyāsī*. During these travels, he got the opportunity to closely associate with many elevated Saints of India, read the writings of the great *Āchāryas* of the past, and reside in many famous holy places.

Ultimately his search took him to the lotus feet of his Spiritual Master, Jagadguru Shree Kripaluji Maharaj (who is lovingly called "Maharajji" by his devotees). He was overawed by the unfathomable scriptural knowledge and ocean of Divine Love that he saw manifest in his Spiritual Master. About this first meeting, Maharajji later remarked, "He recognized me as one would recognize his mother."

Under the guidance of Shree Maharajji, he practiced intense *sādhanā* while residing at the *āśhram*. He also extensively studied the Vedic scriptures, and the Indian and Western systems of philosophy. Upon completion of his studies, his Guru entrusted him with the key task of propagating the ancient knowledge of the Eternal Truth, the world over.

For the last quarter of a century, Shree Swamiji has been traveling far and wide, awakening hundreds of thousands of seekers. Wherever Swamiji goes, he attracts huge audiences. Hearing the profound secrets of the Vedas from him is a rare privilege, for he is able to explain the ancient esoteric knowledge with rigorous scientific logic, in the modern context. Using perfect logic, and a simple-yet-scientific approach, Swamiji offers new ways of understanding and applying the knowledge of the scriptures in our daily lives. The hallmark of his lectures is the ease with which he dispels various myths and misnomers associated with the various paths of God-realization, and his ability to penetrate even the toughest minds and convince them with depth of understanding and scriptural veracity.

Swamiji's lectures cover the teachings of the Vedas, Upanishads, Shreemad Bhagavatam, *Purāṇas*, Bhagavad Geeta, Ramayan, and other Eastern scriptures and Western philosophies. Like the true Disciple of a true Master, Swamiji masterfully quotes from the scriptures of all the great religions, to satisfy even the most discerning of knowledge-seekers. He also reveals the simple and straightforward path to God-realization that can be practiced by anyone.

Although Swamiji started preaching in India two decades ago, he now preaches both—in India and abroad. He has inspired innumerable devotees in Singapore, Malaysia, and Hong Kong, where his visit is always anxiously awaited. Since 2008, on the instruction of Shree Maharajji, Swamiji has increasingly begun spending more time in USA, where his educational background and command over the English language make his programs particularly charming to the intelligentsia, professionals, and academicians.

Shree Swamiji has founded many organizations in India with permanent centers and *āśhrams*, such as Jagadguru Yog Trust, India, Radha Govind Dham in Delhi, Radha Krishna Bhakti Mandir in Cuttack, Radha Govind Dham in Berhampur, Shyama Shyam Dham in Jajpur, Radha Govind Dham in Parla Khemundi, Radha Govind Dham in Karanjia, etc.

In USA, Swamiji has inspired the formation of Jagadguru Kripaluji Yog, a 501(c)(3) non-profit organization. In the space of a few years, JKYog centers have opened throughout the length and breadth of USA.

Swamiji cares deeply about imparting Hindu cultural and religious values to the younger generation, especially in the West. Towards this end, he has conceived a special Personality Development program for children and young adults. This program is called "The Bal-Mukund Playground for Vedic Wisdom". It includes character building, yog, meditation, devotional singing, and religious training. Many Bal-Mukund centers have been started for the benefit of children, both in USA and in India.

Shree Swamiji has a God-gifted ability to keep all kinds of audiences enthralled and entertained through wisdom-filled anecdotes, humorous stories, and irrefutable logic. He has inspired innumerable people, of all ages, towards the path of God Realization, the world over. Swamiji's warmth and humility touch all those who have the fortune to have his association. In fact, his very presence radiates Grace and Bliss.

# Foreword

While conducting spiritual programs, I have often found the question-and-answer session to be a highly awaited item. People look to it anxiously for removing their inner cobwebs of lingering doubts regarding life, duty, philosophy, and the scriptures. Many a time, resolution of the doubt creates an experience that is nothing short of an epiphany, a sudden enlightenment, or an intuitive leap of realization. The satisfaction of having a troubling question answered after many years of intellectual discomfort is much like the gratification of taking off a tight shoe after wearing it all day, except that the latter is a physical relief while the former is an intellectual deliverance.

Over the last two decades, I have observed the questions follow a repetitive pattern. Throughout the cross-section of society, the basic doubts are often similar. This observation led to the idea of writing this book, and making the discussions available as a reference source for sincere seekers worldwide, who are looking for answers to their own questions.

With this plan, I invited questions through the JKYog Google discussion group, Facebook, and Twitter. The deluge of questions that followed was then filtered, classified, grouped, and finally sequenced in a topical flow. The result is the book "Spiritual Dialectics" that you are holding in your hands.

I wish to convey my heartfelt thanks to all those who generously supplied the questions for this book. Special thanks to the group members who took the pains of putting on their thinking caps and sending as many questions as came to their minds. The criteria for selecting the questions for inclusion in this book were simple: I would ask myself: "Does this question exist in the minds of many people? Have I been asked similar questions multiple times in the past? Would this be of common interest to many readers?"

Many questions had to be left out in the fear of making the book too voluminous. Some questions were not selected because they were not of general interest. In many cases, based on the request of the questioners to maintain anonymity, their names and location were changed. To those whose queries got left out, I do not guarantee an individual reply by email, but I do assure that if you come and meet me at any of my forthcoming program venues, I will make time available to clarify your doubt before or after the program.

I would like to express my gratitude to the members of my Indian team, especially Pragnyan Vaidya, for undertaking various tasks related to the publishing of this book, from proof-reading to typing the Sanskrit and Diacritical fonts. A special thanks to Shreya Bhat of Dallas for going through the text and offering invaluable suggestions. Thanks to Shailee, the master designer of our team for providing the cover design. A special appreciation for Anand and Pankaj, who diligently supervised the composition and the printing process.

I hope the book will fulfill the sincere objective with which it has been written, and help seekers in their quest for the Absolute Truth and their journey to God-realization.

In the service of the Lord,
***Swami Mukundananda***

# The Dialectic Process

Dialectics, in philosophy, is a method of investigating the nature of the Truth, through discussions in the form of questions and answers. We find it repeatedly used by Western philosophers throughout history. Socrates used the dialectic process to instruct his students, and he vigorously encouraged them to question existing beliefs. Plato, his illustrious disciple, adopted the dialectical method in his famous book, "The Dialogues." Another noted Greek philosopher, Aristotle, thought of dialectics as a search for the philosophical basis for science.

In the Western world, the German philosopher Hegel is often considered the father of Dialectics. Hegel believed that the evolution of ideas occurs through a dialectical process—that is, any concept gives rise to its opposite viewpoint. This conflict is then resolved through logical analysis, to reach a synthesis. The synthesis is a higher level of truth than the premises.

Karl Marx applied the concept of dialectics to social and economic processes, and called his theory, "Dialectical Materialism". Immanuel Kant coined the term "Transcendental Dialectic" to express the way to go beyond the constraints of human rationality.

The Dialectic system of analysis of the truth through questions and answers is all the more popular in the Vedic literature. It was the favorite technique of the Avatars of God and great sages for imparting knowledge. The dialogues of these great personalities with their students and disciples have been chronicled in the revealed scriptures, and the consequential reservoir of knowledge created by these discussions has satiated the thirst of innumerable seekers.

The most famous amongst these is the Bhagavad Geeta, which is a dialogue between Arjun and the Supreme Lord Shree Krishna. Seeing his relatives and elders on the opposing side, in the battlefield of Kurukshetra, Arjun was confused about his duty. Shree Krishna imparted Divine knowledge, by answering his questions, to enlighten him with the Absolute Truth.

The great Sage Ved Vyas wrote the Shreemad Bhagavatam entirely in the dialectic form. He included in it a number of dialogues, such as those between Jada Bharat and Rahugan, Vidur and Maitreya, Uddhav and Shree Krishna, etc. Shukadev Paramhans recited the Bhagavatam with all these dialogues to King Parikshit. In that assembly, Suta Goswami was present, and he too heard it from the mouth of Shukadev Paramhans. The Bhagavatam was then recited by Suta Goswami to Shaunak Muni, and he included the question-answers between Shukadev and Parikshit in it. Finally, Ved Vyas again compiled the Bhagavatam, and added to it all the discussions between Suta and Shaunak as well. So the Bhagavatam has five primary dialogues, along with many tertiary ones.

The Dialectic process is also a part of many of the Upanishads. The famous Kathopanishad is a dialogue between Nachiketa and Yamraj. In the Prashnopanishad, the sage Pippalad is questioned by six pupils: 1. Sukesha, the son of Bharadwaja. 2. Satyakama, the son of Shibi. 3. Sauryayani, the descendant of Garg. 4. Kaushalya, the son of Ashwala. 5. Bhargava of the Bhrigu Gotra. 6. Kabandhi, the son of Katya. The discussion with each of them forms a separate chapter of the Upanishad.

Another famous scripture based on the Dialectic process is the *Yog Vāsiṣhṭha*. This is dialogue between Lord Ram and His Spiritual preceptor, Maharishi Vasishtha. The question and answer system also makes up many chapters of the Ramayan, Mahabharat, and many other Vedic scriptures.

The *Khaṇḍan Maṇḍan* Paddhati of lecturing is also based on the Dialectic process. Here, the speaker creates a doubt in the minds of the listeners, and then goes on to resolve it. The idea is that when the curiosity is aroused and then satisfied, the knowledge sinks deep in. Instead, if the knowledge is given without initially creating a doubt in the minds of the listeners, it does not have the same impact.

The Dialectic process, which has been so abundantly used in pedagogy, both in the Eastern and Western hemispheres, is thus the basis of the format of this book.

# Essence of the Philosophy of Divine Love

## The Teaching of

## Jagadguru Shree Kripaluji Maharaj

1. Every living being is incessantly searching for happiness. This search is natural to our being, since we are eternal parts of God, Who is the ocean of Divine Bliss. The search for happiness is unknowingly the search for God. Upon attaining Him alone can the soul experience the unlimited Divine Bliss that it is hankering for. Hence, God-realization is the goal of our lives.
2. We cannot know God by our senses, mind, and intellect. These instruments of knowledge of ours are material, and cannot fathom the Divine nature of the Supreme Being.
3. The only means of knowing God is through His Divine Grace, whereby He Himself bestows His Divine knowledge upon the soul.
4. If we wish to receive that Divine Grace, we must surrender ourselves to Him. This surrender is not an external act, it must be from within. True surrender is that of the mind.
5. The difficulty in surrendering our mind to God is that at present, it is attached to the world; we must first detach it from the world, and only then can we attach it to God.
6. At this stage, we need a Guru, or a Spiritual Master who can explain to us on the basis of the scriptures, how to detach the mind from the world and attach it to God. The qualification of a genuine spiritual Master is that he must be God-realized himself.

7. Although the Vedas mention the three means of *Karm*, *Gyān*, and *Bhakti*, our goal of God-realization can be accomplished through *Bhakti* alone. *Karm* needs the addition of *Bhakti* to make it *Karm Yog*; *Gyān* needs the addition of *Bhakti* to make it *Gyān Yog*; while *Bhakti* is by itself *Bhakti Yog*.

Jagadguru Shree Kripaluji Maharaj

# Guide to Hindi Pronunciation

| | | |
|---|---|---|
| अ | *a* | as *u* in b*u*t |
| आ | *ā* | as *a* in f*a*r |
| इ | *i* | as *i* in p*i*n |
| ई | *ī* | as *i* in mach*i*ne |
| उ | *u* | as *u* in p*u*sh |
| ऊ | *ū* | as *o* in m*o*ve |
| ए | *e* | as *a* in ev*a*de |
| ऐ | *ai* | As *a* in mat; sometimes as *ai* in *ai*sle with the only difference that a should be pronounced as *u* in b*u*t, not as *a* in f*a*r |
| ओ | *o* | as *o* in g*o* |
| औ | *au* | as *o* in pot, or as *aw* in Saw |
| ऋ | *ṛi* | as *r* in *Kṛiṣhṇa* |
| : | *ḥ* | it is a strong aspirate; also lengthens the preceding vowel and occurs only at the end of a word. It is pronounced as a final *h* sound |
| · | *ṁ* | nasalizes and lengthens the preceding vowel and is pronounced as *n* in the French word Bon |
| क | *ka* | as *k* in kite |
| ख | *kha* | as *kha* in Eckhart |
| ग | *ga* | as *g* in goat |
| घ | *gha* | as *gh* in Dig hard |
| ङ | *ṅa* | as *n* in finger |
| च | *cha* | as *cha* in chair |
| छ | *chha* | as *chh* in staunch heart |

| | | |
|---|---|---|
| ज | *ja* | as *j* in jar |
| झ | *jha* | as *dgeh* in Hedgehog |
| ञ | *ña* | as *n* in lunch |
| ट | *ṭa* | as *t* in tub |
| ठ | *ṭha* | as *th* in hothead |
| ड | *ḍa* | as *d* in divine |
| ढ | *ḍha* | as *dh* in Redhead |
| ण | *ṇa* | as *n* in burnt |
| त | *ta* | as *t* in French word matron |
| थ | *tha* | as *th* in ether |
| द | *da* | as *th* in either |
| ध | *dha* | as *dh* in Buddha |
| न | *na* | as *n* in no |
| प | *pa* | as *p* in pink |
| फ | *pha* | as *ph* in Uphill |
| ब | *ba* | as *b* in boy |
| भ | *bha* | as *bh* in abhor |
| म | *ma* | as *m* in man |
| य | *ya* | as *y* in yes |
| र | *ra* | as *r* in remember |
| ल | *la* | as *l* in light |
| व | *va* | as *v* in vine, as *w* in swan |
| श | *śha* | as *sh* in shape |
| स | *sa* | as *s* in sin |
| ष | *ṣha* | as *sh* in show |

| | | |
|---|---|---|
| ह | *ha* | as *h* in hut |
| क्ष | *kṣha* | as *ksh* in freak show |
| ज्ञ | *gya* | as *gy* in big young |
| ड़ | *ṛa* | There is no sign in English to represent the sounds ड़ and ढ. They have been written as *ṛa* and *ṛha*, but the tip of the tongue quickly flaps down. |

# Contents

## 12. Radha Rani



## 13. Secret of God's Descension



## 14. Science of Devotion



## 15. The Guru

## 16. Meditation and *Sādhanā*

## 17. *YOG*

# 1

# Who Are We?

## The Body is a House for the Soul

**Question:** It is often said that we are not the body but the soul. Who are we?

*- Srini Teluru, Chicago, Illinois*

**Answer:** Dear Srini, When we ask the question, "Who am I," we begin our quest for spiritual knowledge. This is the first step. The inscription on the temple of Apollo at Delphi says *Knothi Seuton*, or "Know Thyself". It is said that once Socrates was pondering over philosophic truths and walking absentmindedly on the street, when he bumped into someone. Annoyed, the man asked, "Can you not see where you are walking? Who are you?"

Socrates replied nonchalantly, "My dear friend, I have been pondering over that question for the last forty years, and have still not found the answer. If you have any tips to offer, do let me know."

The Bhagavad Geeta says in this regard:

क्षेत्रक्षेत्रज्ञयोर्ज्ञानं। (भगवद् गीता १३.३)

*kṣhetrakṣhetragyayorgyānaṁ (Bhagavad Geeta 13.3)*

"To understand the difference between the body and the knower of the body is wisdom."

The body is not you; it is like a house in which you reside, or like clothes that you wear. You are the eternal soul seated within it. The body is made from matter, and hence it is perishable, but you, the soul, are Divine, and hence immortal.

*- Swamiji*

## The Soul's Location in the Body

**Question**: Where does the soul reside? Is the soul in us or are we in the soul?

*- Gunjan Pandey, Middletown, Connecticut*

**Answer**: Dear Gunjan, Neither is the soul within us, nor are we in the soul. We are the soul that is seated within the body.

Regarding its place of residence, the Vedic scriptures state that the *ātmā*, or soul, resides in the heart.

हृदि ह्येष आत्मा। (प्रश्नोपनिषद् ३.६)

*hṛidi hyeṣha ātmā (Praśhnopaniṣhad 3.6)*

स वा एष आत्मा हृदि... (छान्दोग्य उपनिषद् ८.३.३)

*sa vā eṣha ātmā hṛidi (Chhāndogya Upanishad 8.3.3)*

These Upanishadic *sūtras* state that the soul resides in the region of the heart. However, it is not physically bound to the heart. Often people ask that if the soul resides in the heart, what happens in the case of a heart transplant. Does the soul get extracted from the body along with the heart? No, if a heart transplant takes place, the soul continues to reside in the same location, despite the change of heart.

*- Swamiji*

## Difference between Consciousness and the Soul

**Question:** What is consciousness? How does it differ from or is identical to the so-called "soul"? Are we in consciousness or is consciousness in us? Or is all that exists verily "consciousness"?

*- T. Ramamurthy, Madurai, Tamil Nadu*

**Answer:** Dear Ramamurthy, "Consciousness" is the symptom of life that is manifested by the soul. It is not the soul itself; rather, it is a quality of the soul. This is just as heat and light are manifestations of the fire, but by themselves, they are not the fire.

Everything that exists is verily the energy of God. However, it is not all consciousness. Matter is "insentient" or devoid of consciousness, while the soul is "sentient" or possessing consciousness. This is an important distinction between the soul and matter.

Apart from having consciousness itself, the soul also has the ability to impart consciousness to matter, when it associates with it. Hence, the insentient matter of the body is made sentient by the presence of the soul. As long as the soul resides in the body, the senses, organs, and limbs, all display signs of life. Upon death, when the soul departs, the body is dead matter once again.

*- Swamiji*

## How Dead Matter Receives Consciousness from the Soul

**Question**: If the soul resides in one place within the body, how can it make the entire body conscious? If consciousness is a quality of the soul, kindly explain how it is passed on to the body?

*- Sirjana Shreshta, Asheville, North Carolina*

**Answer:** Dear Sirjana, Ved Vyas has replied to the first question as follows:

अविरोधश्चन्दनवत्। (ब्रह्म सूत्र २.३.२३)

*avirodhaśhchandanavat (Brahm Sūtra 2.3.23)*

"Sandalwood possesses such a property that if you apply it to the forehead, it cools the entire body. Similarly, the soul, although residing locally in the heart, permeates its consciousness throughout the body."

The second question regarding how consciousness is passed from the soul to the body, has also been answered by Ved Vyas himself:

व्यक्तिरेको गन्धन्वत्। (ब्रह्म सूत्र २.३.२६)

*vyaktireko gandhanvat (Brahm Sūtra 2.3.26)*

"A flower carries aroma itself, and the garden where it grows also becomes aromatic by its presence."

Likewise, the soul is sentient, and by its presence, it makes the dead matter of the body sentient as well.

- *Swamiji*

## Size of the Soul

**Question:** Please clarify about the size of the soul. If it does not have physical boundaries in terms of height and width, how do you separate one soul from another?

- *Ashutosh Tripathy, Minneapolis, Minnesota*

**Answer:** Dear Ashutosh, The soul does not have physical boundaries, since it is formless. But this does not mean that the soul is indistinguishable from other souls. Each soul resides in a different body; each soul has a different personality, existence, karmas, and destiny, which are associated with it.

On the subject of the size of the soul, Indian philosophers present three divergent views:

1. Some say that the soul is *vibhu*, or infinite, because it is non-different from its source, God, Who is infinite.
2. Others say that the soul is *madhyamākār*, or medium-sized.
3. Yet others claim that it is *aṇu*, or tiny in size.

Now let us consider each of these views. First, is the soul infinite in size? No, for had this been so, there would not have been any question of going to heaven or hell after death; we would have existed everywhere; simultaneously; at all times. Our soul would have encompassed the earth, heaven, and hell, and there would be no need to go and come from anywhere.

However, the Vedas state:

पुण्येन पुण्यं लोकं नयति पापेन पापमुभाभ्यामेव मनुष्यलोकम्।
(प्रश्नोपनिषद् ३.७)

*puṇyena puṇya lokaṁ nayati pāpena pāpamubhābhyāmeva manuṣhyalokam (Praśhnopaniṣhad 3.7)*

"If you do pious deeds, after death you will go to the higher abodes; if you engage in sinful activities, you will be sent to the lower planes of existence; and if you engage in both kinds of activities, in your next life you will come back to the earth planet." This Vedic *mantra* negates the possibility that we are infinite in size.

Now consider the second view. Is the soul medium-sized? Let us assume the size of the soul is some finite value "X". This means the soul cannot reside in any life form of size less than "X". However, in nature, we see life-forms that vary in size—from the smallest organisms to giant whales. Therefore, the assumption that the size of the soul is a finite value "X" is flawed.

The Jain scriptures are of the view that the soul is finite. They state that the soul is equal to the size of the body. They come to this conclusion because the soul provides consciousness to the entire body. However, if the soul were of the size of the body, the problem would come upon rebirth. Let us say that the soul was in an elephant's body in one life, and hence, equal to the size of the elephant. If in the next life it were put in a pigeon's body, how would such a big soul fit into the tiny pigeon's body?

So only the third option remains: The soul is infinitesimally small. To give us an idea of its size, the Vedas state:

एषोऽणुरात्मा। (मुण्डकोपनिषद् ३.१.९)

*eṣho 'ṇurātmā (Muṇḍakopaniṣhad 3.1.9)*

अणुप्रमाणात्।। (कठोपनिषद् १.२.८)

*aṇupramāṇāt (Kaṭhopaniṣhad 1.2.8)*

The above *mantras* of the Upanishads declare: "The soul is miniscule in size."

*- Swamiji*

# 2

# The Body, Mind & Soul Relationship

## Difference between The Brain and The Mind

**Question:** What is the mind? It cannot be the same as the soul, since the soul is indivisible, impartial, eternal, and *nirguṇ* (formless). And it is definitely not the brain; then what is it?

- *Manoj Bhattaray, Kathmandu, Nepal*

**Answer:** Dear Manoj, The mind is a subtle machine provided along with the body to the soul. It is such a machine that continuously generates thoughts, feelings, ideas, perceptions, and stores knowledge and memories.

The brain is not the mind. The brain is the hardware that the mind uses for its functioning. Someone's brain may get damaged, but the mind may still continue functioning normally. This shows that the mind is distinct from the brain. Again, in the case of plants, they have no brain, and yet they have a mind. Experiments have shown how they respond to the moods of the gardener and speed up or slow down their growth in response. This illustrates that even plants possess a mind.

The brain is made from the gross elements—earth, water, fire, air, and space. On the other hand, the mind is subtler than these gross elements.

The Bhagavad Geeta states:

भूमिरापोऽनलो वायुः खं मनो बुद्धिरेव च।
अहंकार इतीयं मे भिन्ना प्रकृतिरष्टधा।। (भगवद् गीता ७.४)

*bhūmirāpo 'nalo vāyuḥ khaṁ mano buddhireva cha*
*ahankāra itīyaṁ me bhinnā prakṛitiraṣhṭadhā*

*(Bhagavad Geeta 7.4)*

"Earth, water, fire, air, space, mind, intellect, and ego are various constituents of My material energy—Maya." Here, Shree Krishna has enumerated the mind as separate from the five gross elements. Modern science has some idea of the nature of the gross brain, but is yet to comprehend the functioning of the subtle mind.

The mind is thus distinct from the brain. Nevertheless, in figure of speech, often when we say "the mind," it refers together to the mind and the brain.

- *Swamiji*

## The Nature of Thoughts

**Question:** Thoughts are nothing but unrealized acts. If not, what happens to our thoughts once life ends?

- *Binodini Panigrahi, Rourkela, Orissa*

**Answer:** Dear Binodini, Thoughts are not exactly unrealized acts. They are ideas, plans, conceptions, opinions, and feelings produced by the mind. They are bundles of subtle energy that the mind generates. Modern scientific research in the field of Electroencephalography, reveals the variety of alpha, beta, and gamma waves produced by brain activity. It also correlates altered mental states with differences in wave production by the brain.

The Vedic scriptures, since many millennia, have thrown light on thoughts. They emphasize that the thoughts we harbor in our minds are an important facet of our personality. Every thought has an impact on our subtle and physical body. Thus, thought by thought, we forge our destiny, to elevate or degrade ourselves. The essence of spirituality is to control, purify, and elevate our thoughts.

You have asked what will happen to our thoughts at the end of life. The thoughts will naturally cease to exist in the present mind-body. But the seat of the thoughts, the mind, will continue its journey along with the soul, to the next body. And the kind of thoughts that the mind harbored in the present life will impact the kind of birth we will get in the next life.

*- Swamiji*

## Mind, Intellect, *Chitta*, and Ego

**Question:** The Bhagavad Geeta tells us to surrender the mind and intellect to God. But the Pañchadaśhī defines the mind as the cause of bondage and liberation. Shankaracharya talked of four aspects of the inner apparatus—*mana*, *buddhi*, *chitta*, *ahankār*.

How come the inner apparatus has been classified variously as one, two, three, or four entities? Please explain this difference of opinion between the scriptures and Saints. Also, please specify the distinction between the mind and the intellect.

*- Dillip Patel, Dallas, Texas*

**Answer:** Dear Dillip, The mind operates at four levels:

1. Mind. When it creates thoughts, we call it *mana*, or the mind.
2. Intellect. When it analyses and decides, we call it *buddhi*, or intellect.
3. *Chitta*. When it gets attached to an object or person, we call it *chitta*.
4. Ego. When it identifies with the attributes of the body and becomes proud, we call it *ahankār*, or ego.

These are not four separate entities. They are simply four levels of functioning of the one mind. Hence, we may refer to them all together as the mind, or as the mind-intellect, or as the mind-intellect-ego, or as the mind-intellect-*chitta*-ego. They all refer to the same thing.

Various scriptures describe the mind in one of these four ways for the purpose of explaining the concepts presented therein. For example:

- The Pañchadaśhī refers to all four together as the mind, which it holds to be the cause of material bondage.
- In the Bhagavad Geeta, Shree Krishna repeatedly talks of the mind and the intellect as two entities, and emphasizes the need to surrender both to God.
- The Yog Darśhan, while analyzing the different elements of nature, mentions three entities: mind, intellect, and ego.
- Shankaracharya, while explaining the apparatus available to the soul, classifies the mind into four parts: mind, intellect, *chitta*, and ego.

However, they are all referring to the same internal apparatus within us, which is together called *antaḥ karaṇ*, or the mind.

- *Swamiji*

## Link between Body and Soul

**Question:** How does the soul communicate with the elements in our body? Or does it? Where is the connection between the body and the soul?

- *Andrew Wong, Marine Parade, Singapore*

**Answer:** Dear Andrew, Since the soul is Divine, and the body is material, your curiosity is natural—how does the communication between the two take place?

The soul communicates with the body by energizing it with consciousness, or the force of life. Its presence makes the intellect, mind, and body work. This has been explained in detail in the chapter "Who Are We."

Now the reverse communication—how does the body communicate with the soul? The link between the material body and the spiritual soul is established by the ego. In the materially conditioned state, the first covering on the soul is of the ego. The word for ego in Sanskrit is *asmitā*, which means "that which is not." This ego creates a false identity for the soul. Due to it, the soul is under the illusion of being the body, mind, and intellect.

In this illusion that it is the body, the soul identifies with the pleasures and pains of the body. When the senses come in contact with the sense objects, they experience fleeting pleasure. In its mistaken conception of being the body, the soul too experiences this pleasure. However, the experience does not satisfy the soul, which can only be satisfied by Divine Bliss. So the search for pleasure continues.

This is how the two-way communication between the soul and the body-mind-intellect works.

- *Swamiji*

## Administrative Duties of the Soul

**Question:** What are the activities of the soul in the body? Is the soul simply God's "overseer" in each body with no administrative duties?

- *Smita Singh Deo, San Jose, California*

**Answer:** Dear Smita, To enable us to comprehend the administrative position of the soul in the body, the Vedas give the analogy of a chariot:

आत्मानꣳ रथिनं विद्धि शरीरꣳ रथमेव च।
बुद्धिं तु सारथिं विद्धि मनः प्रग्रहमेव च।।
इन्द्रियाणि हयानाहुर्विषयांस्तेषु गोचरान्।
आत्मेन्द्रियमनोयुक्तं भोक्तेत्याहुर्मनीषिणः।।
(कठोपनिषद् १.३.३ एवं १.३.४)

*ātmānagvaṁ rathinaṁ viddhi śharīragvaṁ rathameva cha*
*buddhiṁ tu sārathiṁ viddhi manaḥ pragrahameva cha*
*indriyāṇi hayānāhurviṣhayānsteṣhu gocharān*
*ātmendriyamanoyuktaṁ bhoktetyāhurmanīṣhiṇaḥ*
*(Kaṭhopaniṣhad 1.3.3 and 1.3.4)*

The Upanishads say there is a chariot; it has got five horses pulling it; the horses have reins in their mouths; the reins are in the hands of a charioteer; a passenger is sitting at the back of the chariot.

In this analogy:

- The chariot is the body.
- The horses are the five senses.
- The reins to the mouths of the horses is the mind.
- The charioteer is the intellect.
- The passenger seated behind is the soul residing in the body.

Ideally, the passenger should give directions to the charioteer, who should accordingly pull the reins and guide the horses in the proper direction. However in this case, the passenger, or the soul is asleep, and so the chariot is going awry:

- The senses (horses) desire to see, taste, touch, feel, and smell various things.
- The mind (reins), rather than controlling the senses, supports their desires.
- The intellect (charioteer), instead of directing where to go, submits to the pulls of the senses.
- Seated on this chariot, the soul (passenger) is moving around in this material world since eternity.

So in the materially bound state, your suspicion is right. The soul does not perform any administrative functions because it has surrendered the control of the chariot. It merely experiences the pleasures of the mind and senses vicariously, by identifying with the bodily elements. And because of its inherent nature to seek the Divine Bliss of God, it perceives the dissatisfaction from bodily pleasures.

However, if the soul wakes up and decides to take a proactive role, it can inspire the intellect in the right direction. The intellect will then govern the mind, the mind will control the senses, and the chariot will move in the direction of eternal welfare.

- *Swamiji*

## The Soul is Responsible for the Actions of the Body

**Question:** According to Bhagavad Geeta 13.30, 13.32, the mind and body do the work, not the soul, which is *akarmī*, only a witness. If we (souls) do not do anything, then why do we have to suffer for all bad karmas and travel through 8.4 million species?

- *Milind Jhakhar, Faridabad, Haryana*

**Answer:** Dear Milind, The soul by itself is not the doer of actions. However, it has been given a body-mind-intellect mechanism by God. These are all made from inert matter, and it is the soul that inspires life into them by its presence. Hence, it is responsible for the actions performed by the body in which it is housed.

This is just as when you sit in a car and drive it, you are responsible for its motion. If the car were to have an accident, the law would not hold the tires, steering wheel, accelerator, or ignition switch liable for it. It would be your responsibility, since you were the driver within. Similarly, the soul seated within the body is held responsible for all the actions of the body-mind mechanism that has been given to it.

There is a story on responsibility in the *Purāṇas*. A king had gone for war on his chariot. While returning from a successful combat, a child got crushed under the wheels of the chariot. The king said, "O Charioteer! You are responsible for this death, since you were driving it at great speed." The charioteer said, "O King! You are responsible for this death, not me. The credit of the successful combat has gone to you, and so the sin is also yours."

- *Swamiji*

# 3

# Rebirth

## Concept of Rebirth

**Question:** Every so often, we read examples of reincarnation, where someone got born again in some other place, after death. Can this be true? What is reincarnation?

*- Brenda Whitney, Ventura County, California*

**Answer:** Dear Brenda, Since the soul is eternal; it is neither born nor does it die. What we call death is the soul leaving the body that had become too dysfunctional and uninhabitable for it. The soul is then given a new body to continue on its journey. This changing of bodies by the soul is called reincarnation.

The Bhagavad Geeta explains this in a very wonderful way:

देहिनोऽस्मिन्यथा देहे कौमारं यौवनं जरा।
तथा देहान्तरप्राप्तिर्धीरस्तत्र न मुह्यति।। (भगवद् गीता २.१३)

*dehino 'sminyathā dehe kaumāraṁ yauvanaṁ jarā*
*tathā dehāntaraprāptirdhīrastatra na muhyati*

*(Bhagavad Geeta 2.13)*

"The soul changes bodies in this life itself, from childhood to youth, to old age. Similarly, at the time of death, the soul changes bodies. The wise are not bewildered by it."

*- Swamiji*

## Proof of Rebirth

**Question:** The Western world believes that this is the only life we have, and the religions that have originated in India say that we keep taking births, until we are liberated from Maya. Since we have not seen the past or future lives, how can we be sure that the concept of rebirth is correct?

- *Graciela Aribald, Manhattan, New York*

**Answer:** Dear Graciela, The *Nyāya Darśhan* gives the following proof of rebirth:

जातस्य हर्षभयशोकसम्प्रतिपत्तेः। (न्याय दर्शन ३.१.१८)

*jātasya harṣhabhayaśhokasampratipatteḥ*

*(Nyāya Darśhan 3.1.18)*

It says if you observe a little baby, you will find that without any apparent reason it sometimes becomes happy, sometimes sad, and sometimes fearful. The *Nyāya Darśhan* explains that the little baby is remembering its past life, and hence experiencing these emotions.

The *Nyāya Darśhan* gives another proof of rebirth:

स्तन्याभिलाषात्। (न्याय दर्शन ३.१.२१)

*stanyābhilāṣhāt (Nyāya Darśhan 3.1.21)*

It says that a new born baby has no knowledge of language. How can a mother teach it to suckle the breast when it is inserted in its mouth? However, the baby has experience of drinking milk from the breasts, teats, and udders of innumerable mothers in infinite past lives, even in animal forms. Hence, when the mother puts her breast in the baby's mouth, it automatically starts suckling from past practice.

Without accepting the concept of rebirth, it is impossible to explain the disparity between human beings. For example, let us suppose someone is blind from birth. If that person were to ask you, what did he do that he was punished in this way, what answer would you give him? If you said it was the result of his karmas, he would respond that if there was no previous life then there were no past karmas at the time of birth. If you said that it was the will of God, he would reply that if God is all-Merciful, why would He want someone to be blind? The only logical answer would be that the person had had previous lives and it was the consequence of that person's karmas from past lives.

Most of the Eastern religions accept the principle of rebirth. Actually, many famous intellectuals and thinkers in the Western hemisphere have also believed in it, for example Socrates, Plato, Aristotle, Plotinus, Schelling, James Frazer, Henry Jones, Kant, and Renan.

Most early Christians accepted it, but in the sixth century, in the Council that took place, King Justinian rejected the concept of rebirth, and took out all reference to it. He banned belief in it, and said that those who mention it will be punished.

The Sufi tradition of Islam believes in rebirth. The famous Sufi Saint Maulana Jalaluddin Rumi said: "I have had many many births before I became human." Ahmed bin Savit, Ahmed bin Yavoos, Abu Muslim, Khurasani, are other Sufi Saints who have also talked about rebirth.

Also, the Shias amongst the Muslims believe that the soul is born repeatedly.

- *Swamiji*

## Remembrance of Past Lives

**Question:** When we have lived on this earth in past lives, is there any way of knowing what we were? And why do we forget them in the first place? Why did God not design a world where we could remember the past life? If I could know what I did in the past, I could gain from the experience in this life?

- *Harshadbhai Shah, San Antonio, Texas*

**Answer:** Dear Harshadbhai, Memories of past lives are wiped out in the process of death and then rebirth. It is said that death and birth are such painful experiences for the soul that they erase memories of the previous life. Some residual memories do remain, but usually not for long. As the child grows up, the impressions of the present life are so strong that they erase lingering memories of the past life.

If God's design had been different, and we could have remembered our past lives, we could not have lived normally in the present. If a child could remember that he was his mother's grandfather in his previous life, how would he behave like her child?

However, there are exceptions to the rule. Occasionally, there are children who continue to remember their past life even as they grow up. Their statements about their previous lives have been corroborated by scientific investigations.

A British scientist, Harry Price, did research on this for fifty years. He then presented evidence about rebirth in his book "Fifty Years of Psychical Research." Another scientist, Dr. Richards, has also given many evidences in his book, "Thirty Years of Psychical Research."

An American scientist, Professor Stevenson, came to India three times to check evidences. He wrote that he came across actual cases of children who remembered their previous lives. In fact, such children have existed in all cultures, even in countries that are primarily atheistic. Here are the names of a few such children whose statements regarding their previous life have been investigated and found to be true:

| | | |
|---|---|---|
| Cuba | : | Rachale Grande |
| USA | : | Rosenberg |
| Japan | : | Katsu Gori |
| France | : | Thirijage |
| Austria | : | Alexandrana Samona |
| Australia | : | Earnest Brig |
| Denmark | : | Luna |
| Brazil | : | Paulo Lauren |

| | | |
|---|---|---|
| Sri Lanka | : | Ruby |
| India | : | Karimulla |
| Turkey | : | Ismail |
| Lebonan | : | Ahmed Elaver |

*- Swamiji*

## How the Next Birth is Decided

**Question:** The Bhagavatam teaches us that the human birth is very rare. The Ramayan also says the same thing. How is the next birth decided, and what should we do to get a human birth again in our next life?

*- Nityananda Panda, Berhampur, Orissa*

**Answer:** Dear Nityananda, There are 8.4 million species of life in existence. In the species below human beings—animals, birds, fishes, insects, birds, etc.—there is no free will. Hence, upon death the soul is naturally and sequentially promoted to the next species. But human beings possess the free will to act according to their volition, and hence, they are responsible for their actions. Their next birth is decided by their karmas in the present life.

The facility to do karmas is given to the human species, not for animal-like activities, but for God-realization. The scriptures state:

आहार निद्रा भय मैथुनमं च सामान्यमेतत् पशुभिर्नराणाम्।

*āhāra nidrā bhaya maithunaṁ cha sāmānyametat paśhubhirnarāṇām (Hitopadeśha)*

"Eating, sleeping, defending, and mating are activities that animals can do as well as humans." The human form is special because in it we can attain God. If however, some human being focuses his or her consciousness merely on eating, then the body of a pig becomes more suitable for such a person, and the soul is allotted that body in its next life. If someone makes sleeping the goal of life, God says that the body of a polar bear is more suitable for such a consciousness and allots it in the next life. In this manner, one of the factors determining our next birth is our consciousness at the time of death.

Another factor determining our next life is the Law of Karma.

The *Garuḍ Purāṇa* states:

ऊर्ध्वागतिस्तु धर्मेण अधर्मेण ह्यधोगतिः। (गरुड़ पुराण)
*ūrdhvāgatistu dharmeṇa adharmeṇa hyadhogatiḥ*
*(Garuḍ Purāṇa 2.46.35)*

"One who performs pious deeds goes to the higher abodes in the next life; one who does sinful activities is demoted to the hellish abodes." "As you sow, that shall you also reap" is what the Bible also says.

However, the Law of Karma and the determination of our consciousness are so complex that we cannot analyze and determine our next birth by ourselves. The all-knowing God alone has the ability to determine and allot it to us.

\- *Swamiji*

## When Death Occurs in Coma, What Happens?

**Question:** We have heard that whatever we think at the time of death will decide our birth in our next life. Now in such case, what will happen to someone who has slipped into coma?

\- *Manmath Joshi, Clearwater, Florida*

**Answer:** Dear Manmath, Your question refers to a principle stated in the Geeta:

यं यं वापि स्मरन्भावं त्यजत्यन्ते कलेवरम्।
तं तमेवैति कौन्तेय सदा तद्भावभावितः।। (भगवद् गीता ८.६)
*yaṁ yaṁ vāpi smaranbhāvaṁ tyajatyante kalevaram*
*taṁ tamevaiti kaunteya sadā tadbhāvabhāvitaḥ*
*(Bhagavad Geeta 8.6)*

"Whatever one remembers at the time of leaving the body, one attains the same in the next life."

Death is such a painful experience that it is difficult to focus one's thoughts at that time, and the mind naturally gravitates to whatever one has practiced thinking of throughout one's life. Hence, what we think of at death, reflects the consciousness we cultivate during life.

The verse implies that it is the cultivation of our consciousness during our life, which determines the next birth.

The pain of death is compared to two-thousand scorpions biting the body at the same time. Nobody is able to tolerate such pain, hence the mind and intellect stop functioning, and one falls into unconsciousness. Then death comes. So the fact is that almost everyone slips into a coma before death comes. But the laws of God are not irrational or whimsical. For the sake of making the average human being understand them, they are sometimes explained in simple terms.

So if, for medical reasons, someone slips into coma before death, God will grant the next birth according to that soul's karmas and the consciousness it had cultivated during the present life.

- *Swamiji*

## The Gross, Subtle, and Causal Body

**Question:** You mentioned once that the mind and intellect go along with the soul. What role do they play when the soul takes on a new body?

- *Sosheel Sharma, Kuala Lumpur, Malaysia*

**Answer:** Dear Sosheel, In reply to your question, let me first explain the three kinds of bodies:

1. Gross body: This consists of the five gross elements—earth, water, fire, air, and space.
2. Subtle body: This consists of the eighteen elements—five *prāṇs* (life airs), five working senses, five knowledge senses, mind, intellect, and ego.
3. Causal body: This includes the *sañchit* karmas (the account of our karmas in endless lives).

At the time of death, the soul leaves the gross body behind, but the subtle body and causal body go along with the soul.

स यदा अस्मात् शरीरात् उत्क्रामति।
सः एव एतैः सर्वैः उत्क्रामति।। (वेद)

*sa yadā asmāt sharīrāt utkrāmati*
*saḥ eva etaiḥ sarvaiḥ utkrāmati (Vedas)*

"When the soul departs from the body, the subtle and gross bodies depart with it." So the mind and intellect continue with the soul from life to life. That is the reason why someone who is blind from birth is able to see dreams, since impressions from past lives exist in the subconscious mind.

This also explains why some people have gifted-intellects in certain fields, from their childhood itself. For example, by the age of six, Mozart became an accomplished performer on the clavier, violin, and organ, and was highly skilled in sight-reading and musical improvisation. This was possibly a consequence of the musical IQ developed in his previous life.

At the same time, God adjusts the mind and intellect upon rebirth to make them suitable to the new body. Thus, you would not expect a baby to possess every aspect of the intellect developed in its previous life but the general tendencies are carried forward.

When the material world is annihilated, all the elements of the material energy are absorbed back into God. During *Mahāpralay*, or dissolution the materially bound souls reside in a state of inanimation. In this state, both—the subtle and gross bodies—of all the souls in the material world are destroyed. But the causal body remains, containing information about all past lives. Hence, when God creates the material world again, the souls that were in a state of inanimation again receive subtle and gross bodies according to the information in their causal body.

Upon God-realization, all three bodies are destroyed, and the soul gets a Divine body with Divine mind and intellect, with which it participates in the eternal *leelas* of God in His Divine abode.

- *Swamiji*

# 4

# Free Will vs God is the Doer

## Why the All-loving God Created the Souls

**Question:** Radhey Radhey Swamiji, It is really a pleasure listening to you, and thank you very much for giving us such deep knowledge in simple language so that souls like us can understand it. My question is, why did God create souls and bring us into the world, where there is so much of suffering and misery?"

- *Saurabh Johri, Irving, California*

**Answer:** Dear Saurabh, Radhey Radhey. To answer your question, let me tell you a story. There was once a very rich man, who had a fifteen-year old son. One day, the son was alone in his father's office, when he saw a fifteen-year old newspaper. It had an article titled, "Billionaire adopts orphan child." The boy was stunned to see his father's name mentioned there. When his father returned, the son accosted him, "Father is this article true?"

The father replied, "My son! It is true."

"Does that mean I am not your child?"

"That is right, you are not my child."

The son was shocked. "Then why did you adopt me?"

The father explained, "Son, I am a billionaire. I had no shortage of money, and everything that money could buy. However, I did not have anyone with whom I could share my wealth. I adopted you so that I could give you everything I possess."

Similarly, God is perfect and complete in Himself, and the possessor of unlimited opulences. He creates us so that He may be able to share all that He possesses with us. However, He can only do so when we truly love Him.

Those souls, who have learnt to love God, are with Him in His eternal abode. We conditioned souls are here in the material realm because we have turned our backs towards Him. God hopes and waits for the day when we too will perfect our love for Him and attain Him for the rest of eternity.

*- Swamiji*

## We Suffer because We Have Chosen Maya

**Question:** Dear Swamiji, We are the part of Supreme soul… purest of all. Still…why do we commit mistakes?

*- Pitamber Maharana, Bhubaneshwar, Odisha*

**Answer:** Dear Pitamber, A drop, which is a part of the ocean, possesses many of the qualities of the ocean. Like the ocean, it contains water with salts dissolved in it. Similarly, we are all parts of the Lord, who is Supremely pure, as you have mentioned, and hence we too possess His purity. We souls are Divine, just as God is Divine.

However, as fragments of God, we also possess another quality of His. That is the freedom to act as we wish. God is *abhigya svarāṭ*, supremely independent. We too possess this independence, but to a smaller extent. We are not machines created by Him; we have been made as individual personalities, possessing the privilege to decide our actions.

This privilege gives us the option to either choose God, or the world. The problem is that we have utilized our independence to turn away from God, towards Maya. Consequently, the illusory energy,

Maya, has overcome us and put us in ignorance. It is because of the covering of ignorance that we make mistakes.

*- Swamiji*

## We Have the Free Will to Act

**Question:** When God is the actual Doer, why are the souls subjected to the results of their karmas?

*- Rajesh Kumar Tiwari, Yamuna Vihar, Delhi*

**Answer:** Dear Rajesh, Many people diminish the need for self-effort in their minds by saying, "Nothing is in our hands. God is seated within us. He is the doer of all our actions, and we act as He inspires us." However, this philosophy is not really true, as the following points will illustrate:

1. If God were the doer of all our actions, we would never have committed any mistakes. All of our works would have been perfect, since God can never make a blunder. The fact that we make innumerable mistakes implies that we are performing actions with our own free will.
2. If God were the doer of our actions, we would not have to bear the karmic reactions. Why would we suffer for works that God did through us? He would either bear the karmic reactions on His own, or forgive Himself. But there is the Law of Karma, "As you do, so you shall reap." This implies that we ourselves are responsible for what we do.
3. God is impartial towards all souls and perfectly just. If He was the doer of our actions, He would either have made everyone do good works and become Saints; or He would have made everyone do bad works and become demons. But there is so much of variety in the world. One is a Saint, like Prahlad, while the other is a demon, like Hiranyakashipu. This variety implies that we have the freedom to choose our own actions, and we are responsible for them, not God.

4. If God were the inspirer of our actions, there would be no need for Him to reveal the Vedas or any other scriptures. There would be no need for Him to explain to us the path to perfection. He would simply have to say two sentences: "O souls, I am the doer of everything. So you do not have to understand what proper and improper action is."

It is true that God is seated within us, and He gives us the power to act. However, what we do with that power is decided by our own free will. This is just as the powerhouse supplies electricity to your house. If it did not give the power, you would not have been able to use any electric appliances in your home. However, once you do have that power, what you do with it, is your own choice. You could operate the fan, light the lamp, or heat/cool the house, as you wish.

Similarly, God gives our eyes the power to see. If He did not give us this power, we would not have been able to see anything. But once we do have this power, what we see is in our own hands. You could go to the temple and see the Deities, or you could see dirty pictures on the internet. God is merely giving you the power to see. What you decide to see is your own choice decided by your free will.

Hence, we must not blame God for our mistakes. If we do something wrong, we should take responsibility for the error and strive to correct it.

- *Swamiji*

## God's Responsibility in Our Actions

**Question:** Respected Swamiji, I have heard you explain in your discourses that we souls are the doers of our actions. Then why have the *Bhakti* Saints written *padas* (devotional songs), saying that they are only instruments in the hands of God, and that He is a real doer of their karmas?

- *Amit Mehta, Gujarat*

**Answer:** Dear Amit, The concepts *Karm* (action) and *Karmphal* (fruit of those actions) need to be understood separately for two categories—before surrender to God and after surrender to God.

Consider the first category—those souls who have not surrendered to God. They are under the grip of the unforgiving ego that makes them feel they are the doers. Also, they harbor personal desires independent of the will of God. In this state, God does not inspire their actions. He gives them the power to act, notes their karmas, and gives the fruits at the appropriate time. This has been explained in detail in the previous answer.

Now consider the second category—those souls who are surrendered to the Almighty. They are free from the pride of doership. Also, they make God's desire as their own desire. In this state, the soul becomes the non-doer, and God becomes the Director for that surrendered soul. Hence, the God-realized souls are able to say:

न मै किया न करि सकौं साहिब कर्ता मोर।
करत करावत आप हैं तुलसी तुलसी शोर।।

*na mai kiyā na kari sakauñ sāhiba kartā mora*
*karata karāvata āpa haiñ tulasī tulasī śhora*

The Saint Tulsidas says: "I neither wrote the Ramayan, nor do I have the ability to write it. Shree Ram was the writer Himself, yet people say that Tulsidas has done it." We must bear in mind that this statement applies only to the second category, i.e. the God-realized saints.

The path for moving from the first category to the second category is to perform actions as if they are dependent upon us, and at the same time, to internally practice to think that God is the doer. Sage Vasishtha has expressed this very beautifully, in his advice to Lord Ram:

कर्ता बहिर्कर्तान्तर विहर राघव। (योग वासिष्ठ)

*kartā bahirkartāntara vihara rāghava (Yog Vāsiṣhṭha)*

"O Ram! Act carefully, as if the results are dependent upon You. But from within, practice thinking that God is the real doer." So at present, we will have to keep both principles in mind, as we journey from the materially bound state to the God-realized state.

\- *Swamiji*

## Free Will is Necessary for Love

**Question:** If God had not given us any free will, He could have forced us all to love Him. Then there would be no scope for bondage in the world of Maya. Why did He create Maya and let us have other options?

- *Umesh Vazirani, Cambridge, Massachusetts*

**Answer:** Dear Umesh, Love is only possible where there is an option to choose from. A machine cannot love; a template cannot love. They have no choice. The emotion of love is only possible for someone who possesses a free will.

The presence of Maya gives us souls various options. When we reject Maya in favor of God, we express our love for Him. In fact, the more difficult the choice, the higher is the quality of love possible. Similarly, the more attractive the temptation of Maya, the more is the opportunity for us to express our love for God, by rejecting the temptations and choosing Him. Raman Maharshi was asked, "Why did God create Maya?" He answered, "To thicken the plot."

The presence of Maya is thus essential for the soul to learn love for God.

- *Swamiji*

## Maya's Role in Our Bad Karmas

**Question:** Who encourages the mind to do all bad karmas? Is it Maya? If yes, then why? Please elaborate on these questions.

- *Vinod Kumar Singh, Faridabad, Haryana*

**Answer:** Dear Vinod, The material energy, Maya, definitely presents an option for the soul to act in forgetfulness of God. But at the same time, Maya plays another role as well. When we are allured by its temptations and endeavor to embrace it, Maya punishes us and gives us distress. In this manner, it teaches us to love God and nothing else.

Although Maya does offer temptations for us to indulge in, it is not an enemy of God. The Ramayan says:

सो दासी रघुबीर की समुझें मिथ्या सोपि।
छूट न राम कृपा बिनु नाथ कहउँ पद रोपि।। (रामायण)

*so dāsī raghubīra kī samujheñ mithyā sopi*
*chhūṭa na rāma kṛipā binu nātha kahauñ pada ropi (Ramayan)*

Maya is a servant of God, and its service is to torment souls who are forgetful of Him. Hence, Maya will only release us when we surrender to its Master, Shree Krishna.

- *Swamiji*

# 5

# How to Deal with the World

## No Happiness in the World

**Question:** My question is about how to teach and train mind that there is no happiness in the material world. My mind is revolting while accepting that there is no happiness in material things. Is it OK for us to go through these circumstances and get realization that there is no happiness? For example, there is no happiness in consuming alcohol. So, is it OK if we first test alcohol and then realize that there is no happiness in it? Without going through something how we will know that there is no happiness in it?

- *Natubhai Shah, Toronto, Ontario*

**Answer:** Dear Natubhai, There are innumerable things in the world, and each thing has endless varieties. If you adopt the modus operandi of experiencing everything first before deciding that there is no happiness in it, your whole life will pass in the endeavor. Besides, is there any formula regarding how long you will consume alcohol before coming to the conclusion that it does not give pleasure? There are people who run after money all their lives, and yet do not decide that it does not have the happiness they are seeking. Again, if you finally do come to the conclusion that the world is not a place of happiness, but the mind doubts whether or not there is happiness in

God, then what will you do? You wouldn't be able to demand to see and experience God before concluding that He is an ocean of Divine Bliss.

As human beings, God has bestowed us with subtle intellects that can make this decision even without experience. Broadly, the intellects of living beings can be classified into four categories:

- The lowest is the intellect of an insect. It is attracted to the fire. On coming near the flame, it gets burnt. But it does not learn from the experience, and commits the same mistake repeatedly.
- The intellect of a cat is subtler. If it sits on a hot plate, it learns from its experience. In future, it refuses even to sit on a cold plate, in apprehension that it may get burnt.
- The intellect of a sheep is even subtler. It has never been attacked by a wolf. But the moment it sees a wolf, it perceives impending danger and runs for its life.
- The intellect of humans is even subtler. Merely by intellectual discrimination, without seeing or experiencing, they are expected to reach the conclusion that there is no happiness in the world.

Actually, everyone has had experience of the world to a lesser or greater extent. We made the desires of the senses and strived hard to satisfy them. What was the experience each time? For a moment the desire was quenched, but then it arose again with redoubled intensity. This is the nature of all worldly desires, whether they are the teeny-weeny cravings that you have made innumerable times in your lives or the bigger desires that loom more largely on your mind. The principle is exactly the same. So we should utilize our experience to date, to reach a blanket conclusion about the nature of all worldly desires. That is what God expects us to do, and that is the instruction of the scriptures.

उपासते पुरुषं ये ह्यकामास्ते शुक्रमेतदतिवर्तन्ति धीराः।।
(मुण्डकोपनिषद् ३.२.१)

*upāsate puruṣhaṁ ye hyakāmāste*
*śhukrametadativartanti dhīrāḥ (Muṇḍakopaniṣhad 3.2.1)*

"One who engages in devotion to God, giving up worldly desires, crosses over the ocean of life and death."

- *Swamiji*

## Disturbance from the Behavior of Others

**Question:** I have a very sensitive nature. When anyone criticizes me or gets annoyed with me, it disturbs me to no end; so much so, that sometimes the whole day is spent in brooding. How can I insulate my mood from fluctuations based on the behavior of others?

- *Mahendra Ragoonanan, Port Louis, Trinidad*

**Answer:** Dear Mahendra, the solution is to develop a better understanding of the world, based on scriptural knowledge. The Vedas say that this material energy, Maya, consists of three *guṇas*: *sattva guṇa*, or the mode of goodness, *rajo guṇa*, or the mode of passion, and *tamo guṇa*, or the mode of ignorance.

Everyone's mind too is made from Maya, and so the three modes of Maya exist in the mind as well. Depending upon the environment and where we focus our thoughts, one of the *guṇas* becomes prominent and our mind takes on that quality.

If *sattva guṇa* dominates, one becomes peaceful, contented, generous, kind, helpful, and serene. When *rajo guṇa* gains prominence, one becomes passionate, agitated, ambitious, envious of others' success, and desirous for sense pleasures. When *tamo guṇa* becomes prominent, one is overcome by sleep, laziness, hatred, anger, resentment, violence, and doubt.

For example, let us suppose you are sitting in your library, engaged in study. There is no worldly disturbance, and your mind has become *sāttvic*. After finishing your study, you sit in your drawing room and switch on the television. Seeing all the imagery makes your mind *rājasic*, and increases your hankering for sense pleasures. While you are watching your favorite channel, your family member comes and changes the channel to her liking. This disturbance causes *tamo guṇa* to develop in your mind, and you are filled with anger. In this way, the mind sways between the three *guṇas*, and takes on the corresponding qualities.

This fluctuation takes place constantly in everyone's minds, altering their thoughts amongst the three modes. When two people's *guṇas* are divergent, their ideas, interests, desires, and tastes also become divergent, and that causes strife. This strife exists everywhere, between husband-wife, father-son, brother-sister, friend-companion, and so on. Congruence can happen only when two people have the same *guṇas*. However, since everyone's *guṇas* are fluctuating, it is unreasonable to expect that the other person's *guṇas* will constantly match ours.

The reason for our anxiety is that we have unreasonable expectations. We want others to always think in the same manner as we do. And when this does not happen, we get disturbed. Instead if we could realize that invariably people will have views differing from ours, and this is very natural due to the three modes of material nature, we will not be disturbed when they oppose us or criticize us.

So by increasing our understanding of the world, we can insulate ourselves from the fluctuating moods of others.

- *Swamiji*

## Relationships with Others

**Question:** I am fond of hearing the lectures of saints through the TV channels. Mostly, they all teach us to develop our relationship with God and detach ourselves from the world. My question is why shouldn't we love father, mother, wife, and children, since God is sitting in them?

- *Ganapathy Ramakrishna Prasad, Hayward, California*

**Answer:** Dear Ganapathy, You must first of all understand that you are not the body; you are the soul, and hence your eternal relationship is with God. The worldly relationships are all temporary, and will cease at the end of this life, or even before. You have had unlimited such relatives in your endless past lives. At present, you have no information where the relatives from previous lives have gone. Similarly, your relatives of this life will also leave you one day, and go wherever their karmas determine. But God is eternally seated in your heart, and does not leave you for even a minute. He is your eternal Father, Mother, Friend, and Master, and that is why the scriptures and Saints teach us to love Him and develop our eternal relationship with Him.

Besides, the irrevocable principle of the Bhagavad Geeta is that wherever we attach our mind, that is what we will attain after death. If we attach our mind to the world, we will continue to rotate in the cycle of life and death; and if we learn to love God, we will attain His eternal service in His Divine abode. So the goal of spiritual practice is to detach the mind from the world, and attach it to God.

Once we are established in the platform of love for God, we will then see everyone as parts of the Lord, and experience oceanic love towards all living beings. Our love for others will be pure love, on the platform of knowledge; it will be liberating, not binding. However, the way to reach that platform is to first practice detaching the mind from the world and attaching it to God. At present, if we try to love worldly relatives, it will be on the platform of ignorance—we will see them as are our bodily relatives and be attached to them as such. That will further increase our illusion of being the body. Hence, learning to detach ourselves from worldly relatives is an important aspect of spiritual *sādhanā*.

- *Swamiji*

## Being Compassionate Even When Detached

**Question:** My *sādhanā* has somewhat of an adverse effect on my relationships with others in the material world. I feel that in dissolving my attachment to others, I lose my compassion for them as well. I expect them also to be detached and forget about me and spend their time doing *sādhanā* instead—this results in them getting hurt by my cold response to their warmth. I am confused as to how to find a good balance—to keep God alone in my heart while developing compassion and caring for all around me?

- *Rajendra Mishra, Jagannath Puri, Orissa*

**Answer:** Dear Rajendra, A teacher is personally detached from her students, and yet she lovingly teaches them. A nurse isn't personally attached to her patients, but she compassionately takes care of them. Similarly, if you dissolve your attachment to others, you can still be compassionate towards them.

A part of that compassion is to not apply the same strict standards of spiritual conformity to them as you do to yourself. Remember that they probably do not possess your level of enlightenment. By the grace of God and Guru, you have understood many spiritual truths, but this Grace has not been bestowed upon them as yet. For yourself, try to be totally detached from worldly relatives, but in your expectations from others, be understanding and kind, if they display attachment.

This attachment and detachment that is talked about is an internal state of the mind. The fact that you are detached from others does not have to reflect in a distortion of your behavior towards them. A marketing representative has no attachment towards customers, and yet puts on his best behavior towards them. Similarly, even while being detached within, you can externally behave kindly and lovingly with others.

Having said this, a word of caution must be given. In the initial stage, when our detachment from worldly relatives is slight, it may be necessary to distance ourselves from them to some extent. Else, external sympathies may result in corresponding increase in internal feelings. If you do distance yourself for the sake of achieving your spiritual goal, it is not wrong.

This question regarding what our duty really is will be discussed in the topic "Duty to Others versus Duty to God (in the Chapter Paths to God-realization)."

- *Swamiji*

## Forgiveness

**Question:** Dear Swamiji, Thank you so much for writing this book and for inviting our queries. I have a question about relationships with other souls while on the spiritual path. My business partner swindled the business, and drove me into the toughest two years of my life. Today I am settled again, but I am unable to forgive him. How to get peace of mind when someone has wronged us to no end?

- *Matthew Lehman, Raleigh, North Carolina*

**Answer:** Dear Matthew, This material world is like the prison house of God; souls who have turned their backs towards Him have been put here. So, we cannot expect the people of this world to behave like Saints. There will always be persons who will come to cheat us, and on some occasions they may even succeed. That is life; we all get cheated once in a while. But the important thing is to learn to take it in our stride. That is where the quality of forgiveness comes in.

If we continue to harbor resentment towards those who have wronged us, we will be unable to progress spiritually. Resentment acts like poison on the mind, filling it with bitterness. And we keep reliving the sour experience within, pinned down to the past. Someone aptly said: "Resentment is like taking poison and waiting for the other person to die."

On the spiritual path we must be careful not to nurture ill feelings towards anyone, realizing that they will harm us more than anyone else. Jagadguru Shree Kripaluji Maharaj says:

भूलिहुँ दुर्भावना कहुँ, हो न सपनेहुँ प्यारे। (साधना करु प्यारे)

*bhūlihuñ durbhāvanā kahuñ, ho na sapanehuñ pyāre*

*(Sādhanā Karu Pyāre)*

"Even in your dreams, do not make the mistake of harboring ill-will towards anyone."

Forgiveness is a sublime personality trait that immediately releases all bitterness from the mind. It is a favor we do, not to the other person, but to ourselves. The lives of saintly people are full of inspiring stories of how they forgave their wrongdoers, and even succeeded in winning them over by their love.

A person made an attempt on the life of Mahatma Gandhi, while he was living in South Africa. Mahatma Gandhi refused to hate the man. He said, "I shall love him, and win his love." One year later, that same man came and apologized to Mahatma Gandhi, and wept for forgiveness. This is the characteristic of great personalities; they refuse to allow their minds to dwell on hatred towards anyone.

- *Swamiji*

## Don't Allow Others to Exploit You

**Question:** You teach us that we should increase our tolerance, but if someone is doing wrong with me, should I practice forgiveness, or should I oppose him and stop the atrocity?

- *N. Ramalingam, Schaumberg, Illinois*

**Answer:** Dear Ramalingam, On the spiritual path, we naturally learn to practice tolerance, forgiveness, and humility. However, this does not mean that we should knowingly allow others to exploit us. The scriptures instruct us to take whatever action is necessary, for protecting ourselves in self-defense, when attacked.

There is a charming story in this regard. In a neighborhood, there lived a venomous and foul-tempered snake. The children of that locality were scared of it to death. The moment they would spy it in the distance, they would run for their lives.

One day, Narad ji happened to come to that neighborhood. As was the snake's habit, he approached Narad ji, with his hood raised menacingly and eyes fiercely red. Narad ji stood his ground peacefully, with a benevolent and serene smile on his face. The snake was astonished. "Everyone runs from me in fear. How come you are not scared of me and what is the secret of your peacefulness?"

Narad ji taught the snake the process of devotion, whereupon the snake became his disciple and began practicing *Bhakti*. He shunned violence, giving up his old ways of scaring the neighborhood children.

Soon the children came to know that the snake was harmless and did not bite anyone. Now their fear vanished. They would not leave it alone. On sighting it, they would bombard it with a battery of stones and sticks. They would even come close and kick it with their heeled shoes. The poor snake was badly bruised.

One year later, Narad ji was visiting that area again. He thought, "Let me see how my disciple is doing." He was dismayed to see the snake badly bruised, with a plaster cast on a portion of his body. "What happened to you, my dear disciple?" he asked.

The snake replied, "O Gurudev, this is the result of the *Bhakti* that you taught me. The people of the world, knowing I will not retaliate, do not let me live peacefully."

Narad ji said, "I asked you to stop biting people, but I did not ask you to stop spreading your hood. Whenever the children attack, you should simply raise your head and hiss loudly; then no one will come near you."

Thenceforth, whenever the children came close to the snake, it would hiss loudly and frighten them all away. Soon, it was living peacefully again. Similarly, on the path of devotion, we should shun actions and thoughts directed at harming others, but we definitely have the right to perform legitimate actions in our self-defense.

- *Swamiji*

## Maintaining Peace of Mind when Relatives are Miserable

**Question:** If your near and dear ones are facing problems, and you have done your level best to resolve them, with no positive results, then what is your duty now? Should you leave it to God and feel that now you have peace?

- *Dr. B.B. Singh, New Delhi*

**Answer:** Dear Dr. Singh, As human beings, we are instructed by the scriptures to help others, and endeavor to mitigate their sufferings. But we must do so in a detached manner, leaving the results to God. As long as we are in material bondage, there will always be misery. We will all grow old, we will all become sick, and we will all die one day. Who can escape these realities of life? So we cannot make anyone totally free from misery.

Apart from this, we all have *sañchit* karmas (the karmas of endless past lives) that create suffering and happiness for us from time-to-time. Not even God violates the Law of Karma. The *Purāṇas* tell us that the *Pāṇḍavs* suffered immensely, even though they were great devotees of Shree Krishna. Arjun was a God-realized Saint, and yet his son Abhimanyu passed away, leaving Uttara a widow. Neither Shree Krishna nor Arjun could prevent the bereavement caused by his death. Then how do we hope to remove anyone's miseries entirely.

Again, suffering is sometimes directly given by God for spiritual progress, to increase one's detachment from the world. The scriptures state:

तं भ्रंशयामि सम्पद्भ्यो यस्य चेच्छाम्यनुग्रहम्।
(श्रीमद् भागवतम् १०.२७.१६)

*taṁ bhranśhayāmi sampadbhyo yasya chechcchāmyanugraham*
*(Shreemad Bhagavatam 10.27.16)*

In this verse, God says: "When I wish to bestow the highest treasure of Divine Love upon someone, I first prepare that person by giving suffering." The Bible states: "God sometimes gives misery in our lives, to turn us away from sin, and seek eternal life." At the level of our thinking, material suffering is bad, but in the Divine plan, it may be necessary for the evolution of the soul.

Even if we are successful in removing someone's material miseries, this is only a very partial and temporary solution—you give food to a hungry person, and after six hours he is hungry again. I am not decrying the need for doing material charity towards society. But that is not the only kind of charity that exists. The highest charity is to help someone attain love for God, and get out of the cycle of life-and-death. The God-realized Saints engage in this Divine charity. They remove the root cause of suffering of the souls, which is forgetfulness of God. If we help the God-realized Saints in their welfare work, we effectively engage in the highest charitable activity we possibly can.

So, if people are close to you, do try to alleviate their material miseries. But at the same time, try to inspire them to strengthen their relationship with God. And most importantly, remember to help others as a matter of duty, and leave the results in the hands of God. If your sincere efforts to assist them do not yield results, do not be disturbed.

- *Swamiji*

6

# Science of Surrender

## Definition of Surrender to God

**Question:** I chant the Brahm Sambandh *mantra* "*Shree Krishnah Sharanam Mama*". But I am not clear what surrender means. Can you please explain what surrender to God is?

\- *Nathji Desai, Nadiad, Gujarat*

**Answer:** Dear Nathji, Just as devotion is a broad term that has been defined from varied perspectives and in innumerable ways by Saints, similarly surrender is also a broad term that encompasses many aspects.

At the very outset, surrender means to give up our independent desire, and to desire in accordance with the Will of the Supreme. A natural corollary of this is to utilize our body, mind, and possessions in the service of God.

Further, surrender is characterized by "*anyāśhrayaṇām tyāgaḥ*," or complete dependence on the grace of God. This involves dissolution of the ego that depends upon crutches such as wealth, position, family, etc., and the development of faith that God alone is our shelter. The classic example of Gajraj is often quoted to highlight this aspect of surrender. As long as he depended upon his own strength, God did not come to help him. And the moment he called out to the Lord with full faith in His grace, Lord Vishnu immediately came to the rescue.

Some scriptures have explained surrender by enumerating six points:

- To desire in accordance with the Will of God.
- Not to desire against the Will of God.
- To have firm faith that He is protecting us.
- To always realize His Grace in all things.
- To feel that all we have, belongs to God and our Guru.
- To give up the ego of having surrendered.

*- Swamiji*

## Obstacles due to Negative *Sanskārs* and *Vāsanās*

**Question:** What stops one from complete surrender? Do one's past negative *sanskārs* and *vāsanās* play a part in determining the level and speed of surrender? How can one overcome one's inherent negativities and make progress towards self-surrender faster?

*- Kamala Tavintharan, Singapore*

**Answer:** Dear Kamala, Surrender is not a one-time procedure. It is not that we surrender once, and we are done with it forever. We have to keep surrendering at every moment. In this process, there are innumerable obstacles. Our mind is made of Maya and it naturally runs towards the world. We need to beat this mind with the intellect. We also have *sanskārs* of past lifetimes that must be countered. And then, we have ignorance or *agyān* within us, which is the source of all the problems.

However, we must not feel disillusioned. Innumerable souls in the past have overcome these obstacles to perfect their surrender to God, and have attained Him; if we endeavor sincerely, we too will be successful.

First, we must illumine our intellect with the spiritual knowledge given to us by our Guru. Then, with this purified intellect we must work on the mind, to detach it from the world and attach it to Names, Forms, Pastimes, Virtues, Abodes, and Saints of God. Along with our sincere efforts, we must pray to God and Guru for help, firmly believing that Their Grace can make us perfect our surrender.

To speed up the process of surrender, we should strengthen the sentiment, "God and Guru alone are mine." When we develop love for God and Guru, surrender becomes natural and automatic. When we reach the state of complete surrender, the feeling "He alone is mine" will always remain in our mind, and all our thoughts and actions will be in consonance with it.

If we can keep increasing our desire to serve, that is also a very potent tool for progress. Jagadguru Shree Kripaluji Maharaj states:

सौ बातन की बात इक, धरु मुरलीधर ध्यान।
बढ़वहु सेवा-वासना, यह सौ ज्ञानन ज्ञान।। (भक्ति शतक ७४)

*sau bātana kī bāta ika, dharu muralīdhara dhyāna*
*baḍhavahu sevā-vāsanā, yaha sau gyānana gyāna*
*(Bhakti Śhatak 74)*

"Fix your mind on Shree Krishna, and keep increasing the desire for *sevā*. This is the most powerful weapon for conquering the mind and Maya."

- *Swamiji*

## Evaluating Our Level of Surrender

**Question:** What determines one's level of surrender? Is there some way of knowing how far we have succeeded in the process?

- *Kamala Tavintharam, Singapore*

**Answer:** Dear Kamala, It is not easy to judge one's level of surrender, since it is such a broad term. Only God and our Guru can truly know how much we have advanced. However, a simple parameter, which can give us some idea, is to see how much our mind has gotten detached from the world and the extent to which it has gotten attached to God. This is a simple rule of thumb to measure our advancement.

Do a reading of yourself. When you suffer reversals in the world, how upset do you become? If you find that earlier, you would keep brooding when someone insulted you, but now you are able to forget it in an hour's time, then you can conclude that you are progressing; your mind is becoming detached from the world, and your spiritual power is increasing; hence, you are able to remain normal in trying circumstances.

Again, analyze how much does your mind yearn for spiritual association. If earlier, whenever you had free time, you wished to spend it in seeing movies, but now you seek opportunities to sing devotional *kīrtans*, it is a sure sign that you are progressing and that your mind is getting attached to the spiritual realm.

- *Swamiji*

## Developing an Intense Aspiration for God

**Question:** How can we inflame our aspiration to traverse the path to God-realization?

- *Deepak Subramanium, Atlanta, Georgia*

**Answer:** Dear Deepak, One of the most important devotional virtues, which will stand you in good stead as you move ahead towards God, is the intensity of your aspiration. A strong aspiration will help you cut through the greatest hindrances as a knife cuts through butter. However, if your aspiration is weak, then every little obstacle will appear like a mountain to you. So, you must endeavor not to remain lukewarm, but to keep the desire for spiritual attainment burning brightly.

How can you inflame your aspiration for God? This requires *chintan*, or contemplation. Repeatedly contemplate upon the Divine knowledge of the scriptures, and the knowledge you have heard from the lotus mouth of your Guru and the Saints. Usually seekers feel great inspiration when they attend the lecture series, but once it is over, they find their enthusiasm waning. The reason for this is that while hearing the lectures, the knowledge remains fresh in their intellect. But then, due to lack of revision, the knowledge starts evaporating, causing a dip in their enthusiasm. *Chintan*, or contemplation about what you have heard and read, is the antidote for this. Such *chintan* will strengthen your decision that your eternal relationship is with God alone. And a strong decision will be your asset to further steps.

The Vedas describe a powerful formula for progressing quickly on the path:

स यथा कामो भवति तत् क्रतुर्भवति यत् क्रतुर्भवति
तत् कर्म कुरुते यत् कर्म कुरुते तदभिसंपद्यते॥
(बृहदारण्यक उपनिषद् ४.४.५)

*sa yathā kāmobhavati tat kraturbhavati yat kraturbhavati*
*tat karma kurute yat karma kurute tadabhisampadyate*
*(Bṛihadāraṇyaka Upanishad 4.4.5)*

"The stronger your decision that attaining God is the goal of your life, the more intense will be your desire to meet Him. And the more intense your desire, the deeper will be your resolve to do the things that take you closer to Him. The deeper your resolve, the harder you will try. The harder you try, the more Grace you will attract, and the closer you will come to Him."

So, appreciate the importance of a strong aspiration on the spiritual path and endeavor to ignite it within yourself. Do your *sādhanā* on a daily basis. Read Jagadguru Shree Kripaluji Maharaj's "*Prem Ras Siddhānt*" regularly in which he has summarized the knowledge of all the Vedic scriptures, watch the lecture DVDs you have procured, and keep revising the knowledge with your intellect.

- *Swamiji*

## Causeless Mercy

**Question:** If God is causelessly merciful, He should bestow His Grace without a cause, i.e. without our having to do anything. If we have to surrender first, and then He bestows His Grace, how is He causelessly merciful?

- *Moon Chan Lai, Houston, Texas*

**Answer:** Dear Moon, The question is simplistic, because surrender itself means to come to a state of doing nothing. Understand this from the example of a newborn baby. She does nothing, and so her mother does all her work. When she grows into a small child, she begins doing some of her tasks on her own, and so her mother lessens her responsibilities. When she grows up further, she begins doing all her works herself, and her mother stops doing everything.

This example is illustrative of the process of surrender. As long as we possess the pride of performing our actions, God declares us as the doer, and we have to suffer the consequences of our actions according to the Law of Karma. When we surrender this pride, we become the non-doer and God becomes the performer of our every action.

तेषां सततयुक्तानां भजतां प्रीतिपूर्वकम्।
ददामि बुद्धियोगं तं येन मामुपयान्ति ते।। (भगवद् गीता १०.१०)

*teṣhāṁ satatayuktānāṁ bhajatāṁ prītipūrvakam*
*dadāmi buddhiyogaṁ taṁ yena māmupayānti te*
*(Bhagavad Geeta 10.10)*

According to this verse from the Bhagavad Geeta, the Supreme Lord takes the responsibility for the welfare and liberation of surrendered souls. Therefore, if simply by giving up the pride of doing, we are liberated from material bondage and rewarded with Divine Bliss, is this not the Causeless Mercy of God?

If we were required to do something to become beneficiaries of His Grace, then we could have had occasion to complain. However, surrender is the process of giving up everything to attain everything. As long as a bird holds a piece of flesh in its beak, other birds chase it and do not allow it to rest in peace. The moment the bird gives up this piece of meat, i.e. surrenders everything, it attains peace. In the same way, surrender involves no effort at all. Without any effort if we receive Divine Grace, then that Grace is definitely causeless.

There is the famous incident of Draupadi's surrender. When Draupadi was being disrobed in the assembly of the *Kauravas*, she first counted upon the protection of her husbands. When they remained silent, she relied upon the pious elders present in the assembly—Dronacharya, Kripacharya, Bhishma, Vidur, etc.—to help her. When they too failed to take any step, she clenched her sari between her teeth. Yet, Shree Krishna did not come to her rescue. Finally, when Dushasan pulled her sari with a jerk, it slipped from her grasp. Now she surrendered herself totally to Shree Krishna, for she no longer had any faith in the protection of others, nor was she relying on her own strength. Immediately Shree Krishna offered complete protection, and she was saved. Shree Krishna declares in the Bhagavad Geeta:

सर्वधर्मान्परित्यज्य मामेकं शरणं व्रज।
अहं त्वां सर्वपापेभ्यो मोक्षयिष्यामि मा शुचः।। (गीता १८.६६)

*sarvadharmānparityajya māmekaṁ śharaṇaṁ vraja*
*ahaṁ tvāṁ sarvapāpebhyo mokṣhayiṣhyāmi mā śhuchaḥ*

*(Bhagavad Geeta 18.66)*

"Abandoning all concerns of religiosity and irreligiosity, simply surrender to Me. Then I, Who dispenses justice to all, will cease to be a mere judge. Bestowing My Grace, I will pardon all the sins of your innumerable past lives, and grant you liberation." This is the immense Grace of God.

In the world, even if a criminal surrenders to the law, he is not absolved of his past crimes; he is made to suffer punishment for them. But God is so merciful that once you surrender to Him, He not only forgives all past deeds, but also bestows His Divine Bliss for the rest of eternity. If this is not causeless Grace, then what is?

If a washer man were to clean your clothes and not charge you for it, you would say that he did you a favor, even though the clothes could become dirty again. In comparison, when we surrender our mind and intellect to God, He cleans them forever, and that too, without any charge. In fact, even if we desire, we can never pay the price for God's Grace. What we receive through Grace is Divine wealth, while what we give in return is only imperfect material goods. What need does God have for our material goods anyway? So, if God bestows His Grace upon our surrendering to Him, it is indeed His causeless mercy.

\- *Swamiji*

## The Unbreakable Rules of God

**Question:** Our concept of God is that He is all-powerful and can do whatever He wishes. When God can do anything, He should also be able to bestow His Grace on us without our surrender. In this way, He should liberate all the souls from the material world. Then why does He require us to fulfill any conditions for bestowing His Grace?

- *Stephen Zamansky, Houston, Texas*

**Answer:** Dear Stephen, This statement that God can do anything needs to be understood carefully. It means He can perform feats that are impossible for us, such as create the world, maintain it, annihilate it, etc. He can even perform contradictory actions, such as simultaneously being formless and possessing a form, being further than the furthest and closer than the closest, being soft as a rose and hard as a thunderbolt, etc.

However, God has His own rules of action that He never breaks. For example, He has a rule:

करम प्रधान विश्व करि राखा।
जो जस करइ सो तस फलु चाखा।। (रामायण)

*karama pradhāna viśhva karī rākhā*
*jo jasa karai so tasa phalu chākhā (Ramayan)*

"The Law of Karma prevails in this world. Whatever you do, you shall reap accordingly." This law has been created by God Himself, and He never breaks it. Thus, we see that Dashrath, the father of the Supreme Lord Shree Ram, passed away; his wife, Kaushalya, became a widow; but Ram did not save His own father. God says, "The rule is the rule. It is immaterial whether someone is My mother or father. This is not a homely affair that the Judge (God) has become a member of the family, and so there will be some concessions. Everyone will get the results according to their karmas." That is why everyone has faith that they can expect justice from God, although worldly people may cheat them, for there cannot be an unfair God.

Similarly, there are innumerable other rules that God never breaks. Jagadguru Shree Kripaluji Maharaj says he could write a book on all the things that God cannot do. Likewise, God has a rule that only if we surrender to Him, we will receive His Grace.

You may say that if this rule did not exist, it would be very advantageous. What would be the advantage? Well, we would not surrender to God and would still receive His Grace. Yes, but the reverse could also be true, that we surrendered to God and still did not receive His Grace. That would be disastrous. So God says that He does not break His rule. If we wish Him to bestow His Grace, we will have to surrender to Him.

*- Swamiji*

## Does God Know When We Will Surrender?

**Question:** If God is all-knowing, He should also know when we will surrender to Him. If He does, then it means that our surrender is decided. Then, where is our free will?

*- John Whitworth, Milwaukee, Wisconsin*

**Answer:** Dear John, God has given us a free-will to do as we wish. But He is expectantly waiting for us to exercise it in His direction, so that He may bestow His Divine Knowledge, Love, and Bliss upon us.

Your logic is correct that if God knew when we would surrender to Him, then it would be a predetermined event, which would mean we had no free will. The fact is that God simply encourages us to surrender, and for this purpose He manifests the scriptures and sends His Saints, but even He does not know when we will surrender. He leaves that decision to us.

*- Swamiji*

# 7

# Karma, Destiny, and Astrology

## The Role of Destiny in our Lives

**Question:** We are all born with a destiny, and this cannot be changed, which is the basic principle of the Law of Karma. Is this understanding correct?

- *Hrima Dixit, Bridgewater, New Jersey*

**Answer:** Dear Hrima, To think that we are bound by our destiny, which cannot be changed, is the doctrine of fatalism. This is how the "fatalism" is defined:

1. Doctrine of fate: The philosophical doctrine according to which all events are fated to happen, so that human beings cannot change their destinies.
2. Belief in all-powerful fate: The belief that people are powerless against fate.
3. Feeling of powerlessness against fate: An attitude of resignation and passivity that results from the belief that people are helpless against fate.

Let us analyze whether this concept of fatalism is correct or not. First of all, let us understand what destiny is:

पूर्वजन्मकृतं कर्म तद्दैवमिति कथ्यते। (हितोपदेश)

*pūrvajanmakṛitaṁ karma taddaivamiti kathyate (Hitopadeśha)*

"The actions we performed in our past lives become our destiny in this life." In other words, destiny is not something that has come down from the heavens or a horoscope chart that is revealed to us by astrologers. We have created our destiny ourselves by actions in past births. This means that we performed actions with our free will in past lifetimes.

Now, we shall use the technique of "Reductio ad absurdum" to disprove fatalism. This is a technique where the statement to be disproved is accepted in the premise. It is then shown to lead to a logical inconsistency.

Let us start with the premise that everything is predestined.

- If we are bound by destiny in this life, and cannot perform actions by our own volition, this rule must apply to our past lives as well. It would mean that in past lives too we were bound by destiny, for the rule must be the same in all lives.
- But if in each life we were bound by destiny, then in which life did we perform independent actions that created that destiny?
- And if in no past life we performed actions with our free will, then how was destiny created?
- Again, if we did actions with our free will in any past life, we can do them now as well.

Thus, we see the premise that everything is predestined, leads to a logical absurdity and is disproved. The scriptures say that it is lazy people who blame destiny for their substandard achievements:

दैव दैव आलसी पुकारा।। (रामायण)

*daiva daiva ālasī pukārā (Ramayan)*

"While working, don't bring destiny into your mind, or it will make you lazy." If you do, you will start running to astrologers to know what your destiny is, rather than focusing on performing your work properly.

It is a fact that there is an element of destiny in our lives. However, we also possess the freedom to act as we wish in the present. This is called *puruśhārth*, or the work we do in the present, by using our freedom of choice. The example is given of a game of cards. The hand that is dealt to a person gets fixed; it cannot be changed. But how one plays with the cards is not fixed. If someone is a good player, he or she may win even with bad cards, while if someone is a bad player, he or she may lose even with good cards.

Similarly, if you were destined to win a jackpot of a million dollars, you will win it. But beyond that it is your self-effort. If you work hard, you could multiply it into ten million dollars, and if you develop profligate habits, you could squander it away in drinking and gambling. That would not be decided by destiny; that would be your own *puruśhārth*, or self-effort.

- *Swamiji*

## Terrorist Attacks and the Law of Karma

**Question:** If all outcomes happen due to one's karma, and God gives the results, when ill befalls people, like the terrorist attack in Mumbai, will it be correct to say, "They deserved it due to past karmas," and blindfold ourselves from the misery of humankind?

- *Damini Nedungadi, Kuala Lumpur, Malaysia*

**Answer:** Dear Damini, The Law of Karma is so complex that it involves multiple factors. Let me explain step-by-step the answer to your question, by first describing the three kinds of karmas: *sañchit*, *prārabdh*, and *kriyamāṇ*.

God has an account of all our karmas in our endless past lives. This is called *sañchit* karmas. At the time of birth, we are given a portion of our *sañchit* karmas, to enjoy or suffer in this life. This is called *prārabdh* karmas. The *prārabdh* is fixed, but within this life, we have a freedom to act, and the actions we perform are called *kriyamāṇ* karmas. The *kriyamāṇ* is not pre-determined; it is in our hands, and can be changed as we wish.

Now, the results we get in life are dependent on a number of factors, including:

1. Our *prārabdh* karmas.
2. Our *kriyamāṇ* karmas.
3. The Will of God.
4. The karma of other people present in that situation.
5. Chance events in which we happen to be present by accident.

Since we humans are not all-knowing, we cannot fully correlate the results we get with the exact causes behind them. Besides we do not even know all our past karmas, to make a perfect correlation.

Now, your question is whether the deaths of the people in the Mumbai terrorist attack were because of their karmas or not. There is no blanket answer to this question. It is possible that they were destined to die, and a matter of chance that they died in a terrorist attack. Else it could be a result of any of the other factors listed above. It is not for human beings to know which of the above five factors were responsible for their deaths.

Even in the aforesaid terrorist attack, many people were miraculously saved. Some were scheduled to attend meetings at those very hotels, but for very strange reasons, they could not reach there on time. Yet others happened to come there, equally accidentally. There are many mysteries in creation that will remain mysteries until we become God-realized. Let us leave the question of who died for what reason to God.

But, merely because we cannot understand the specific reasons for them, we must not neglect efforts to counter social evils such as terrorist attacks. We must put in our best efforts and then leave the results to God. Thus, the Saints teach us:

प्रयत्न में सावधान फल में संतुष्ट।

*prayatna meñ sāvadhāna phala meñ santuṣhṭa*

"Act responsibly, but do not be disturbed if the results are not as you wished."

\- *Swamiji*

## Punishment by Society and the Law of Karma

**Question:** I will be thankful if you please clarify my confusion. Is it necessary for human beings to punish wrong doers? Is it God's work to punish others or is it ours? How can we judge others when we ourselves are flawed, as opposed to God, Who has no flaws?

- *Carlos Barito, Pearland, Texas*

**Answer:** Dear Carlos, Your question is very interesting, and this is the first time I have come across this question. When God is the perfect Judge and Dispenser of justice, then why should humans take these works in their hands?

It is true that God is administering this world, but we should not neglect doing our individual or social duties, with the justification, "I do not need to bother. Let God take care of this." For example, on the prescription slips of doctors, often this phrase is printed: "I treat; He cures." Now someone could ask that if God cures, then what is the need for the doctor to treat; the doctor should simply leave it to God. But that would be irresponsible behavior on the part of the doctor.

Similarly, the world environment has been created by God, and no matter how we despoil it, He can adjust the forces of nature to correct it again, if He so wishes. But the fact that God is the Supreme controller of the environment does not mean that we should not act responsibly to protect it.

God has created the Sun, Moon, Earth, and the temperatures on each of these. He is All-powerful and has the power to raise or lower temperatures at will. Yet, there is so much concern nowadays about global warming. We do not think that it is all in God's hands, and so we should not worry about such issues. If we say that and keep pumping exhaust discharges into the atmosphere, thinking let God take care, it will be irresponsible behavior.

So we humans must act in a responsible and complete manner, covering all aspects of individual and societal duties. While performing actions, we must not leave things to God, rather we should pray to Him to do His works through us. Similarly, in matters of law, society itself needs to punish wrongdoers, and develop wisdom to do it in line with the wishes of God. If the provisions for punishment did not exist in society, many people would have gotten the wrong impression that they can do whatever they wish and get away with it. Hence, judicial, police, and prison systems are all essential parts of any society.

- *Swamiji*

## Faith in Astrology

**Question:** Do you believe in astrology? Do you think planetary aspects affect our life? I cannot say I believe in it one hundred percent, but whenever I face difficulties in life, I tend to run to consult an astrologer just to make me feel better that everything will be all right.

- *Usha Prakash, Cupertino, California*

**Answer:** Dear Usha, The configuration of stars does have a minor influence in our lives. It is a part of God's design for dishing out our *prārabdh*, or the results of our past karmas. The subject of astrology attempts to predict this influence of stars. Regarding astrology, the first thing to bear in mind is that the predictions are only partially accurate, as you have remarked in your question.

The second point is that, we always have the freedom to act in the present. This freedom permits us to change our destiny, with sufficient self-effort. The problem with studying astrology is that it makes us fatalistic. We lose focus on our self-effort, or *puruśhārth*. Hence, Chanakya Pandit said:

निरुत्साहाद्दैवं पतितः।

*nirutsāhāddaivaṁ patitaḥ*

"If you are torpid in your effort, you will fail despite the best of destiny."

उत्साहवतां शत्रवोऽपि वशीभवन्ति।

*utsāhavatāṁ śhatravo 'pi vaśhībhavanti*

"If your endeavor is sufficient, you can transform even bad destiny into success." Thus, rather than allowing the configuration of your stars to linger on your mind, put your heart and soul into your present efforts.

- *Swamiji*

## The Problems with Astrologers' Predictions

**Question:** When the astrologer tells us our destiny, we can prepare ourselves for it. So it seems to be advantageous to know what destiny has in store for us. Isn't it very beneficial to go to astrologers?

- *Kishore Agrawala, Rairangpur, Mayur Bhanj, Orissa*

**Answer:** Dear Kishore, Even if the astrologers' predictions are accurate, they are usually disadvantageous to be told. Let us suppose the astrologer informed you that after two years your business will increase manifold. On hearing this, your natural response will be, "Oh is that so? Then I do not need to work very hard. I am going to succeed in any case." In other words, if you come to know of a good destiny, you will reduce your efforts for success.

Now consider what will happen if the astrologer says that your business will crash after ten years. On hearing this, you will think, "Really, my business is going to crash? O God! what will I do? What will I do? What will I do? ..." Whether the business crashes or not, premature worries will make your heart crash.

In this way, on being told a good destiny, you will become lazy, and on being told a bad destiny, you will become worried. So there is no advantage in knowing your destiny. Whatever is written in it, will come by itself. The present is in your hands, and your duty is to put in your best efforts now. Focus on making your destiny rather than knowing it.

Besides, the astrologers' predictions are only partially accurate. In *Kaliyug*, the present age, there are hardly any expert astrologers. With their rudimentary knowledge, they make guesses. A small portion of their predictions turns out right, and their business keeps running. I remember a joke about this. Khushwant Singh, was the Editor of "Illustrated Weekly" in the 1970's, which was India's number one news magazine at that time. He confessed later that his astrologer, who wrote the Zodiac predictions of the week, had left the job. Thenceforth, for the next three years, Khushwant Singh did not hire another astrologer; he would write the predictions himself. Unaware of this, people would often pay compliments about the accuracy of the astrological predictions of his magazine.

So a good policy is to take the predictions of astrologers with a pinch of salt, and instead focus on your efforts. A famous Urdu poet put it very aptly when he said:

खुदी को कर बुलन्द इतना कि हर तकदीर से पहले,
खुदा खुद बन्दे से पूछे बता तेरी रज़ा क्या है।

*khudī ko kara bulanda itanā ki hara takadīra se pahale,*
*khudā khuda bande se puchhe batā terī razā kyā hai*

"Make your efforts so strong that before giving you the results of your destiny God Himself asks you what you want."

\- *Swamiji*

# 8

# Paths to God-realization

## Liberation from Maya

**Question:** Dear Swamiji, Radhey Radhey. Kindly guide us, how we could be released from this Maya?

- *Sanjeev Tiwari, Vikas Puri, Delhi*

**Answer:** Dear Sanjeev, Radhey Radhey. It is a fact that Maya is giving us innumerable miseries—*ādhyātmik* (due to body and mind), *ādidaivik* (due to environmental reasons), *ādibhautik* (due to other living beings). However, the Bhagavad Geeta gives us the process for obtaining release from them:

मामेव ये प्रपद्यन्ते मायामेतां तरन्ति ते।। (भगवद् गीता ७.१४)

*māmeva ye prapadyante māyāmetāṁ taranti te*

*(Bhagavad Geeta 7.14)*

Shree Krishna says: "If you surrender to Me, you will cross over the ocean of Maya." Similarly, the Ramayan states:

सनमुख होइ जीव मोहि जबहीं।
जन्म कोटि अघ नासहिं तबहीं।। (रामायण)

*sanamukh hoi jīva mohi jabahīñ*
*janma koṭi agha nāsahiñ tabahīñ (Ramayan)*

"The moment the soul turns towards God, the sins of endless

lifetimes are immediately destroyed."

We should not make *Mokṣh* (liberation from Maya) as our goal in life. Rather, we should make *Bhagavad Prāpti* (God-realization) as the goal, and *Mokṣh* will happen automatically. This is just as someone makes removal of poverty as the goal. The other person makes accumulation of wealth as the goal, and poverty is automatically removed when wealth is obtained. Similarly, the intelligent person endeavors not for liberation from Maya, but for God-realization.

- *Swamiji*

## Variety of Paths in Hinduism

**Question:** All the religions of the world describe only one path to God-realization. In Hinduism alone we find so many different approaches, and all of them are accepted as bona fide. This makes it confusing for us. Why did the Vedas not stick to one path?

- *Sunil Kumar, Faridabad, Haryana*

**Answer:** Dear Sunil, Variety is an inseparable part of God's creation. No two leaves of a tree are alike. No two human beings have exactly the same finger prints. Similarly, everybody has different natures too. The variety of paths mentioned in the scriptures accommodates peoples' variegated natures.

As knowledge becomes subtler and more elevated, its branches increase. In Grade Five, students are taught General Science as one subject. But when they reach Grade Seven, Science is divided into three branches—Physics, Chemistry, and Biology. When they reach college, it is further divided into hundreds of branches. And in Graduate School, there are literally thousands of subjects within Science.

Similarly, the Vedas describe spiritual knowledge to sublime heights, and hence the variety of needs of *sādhaks* (spiritual aspirants) gets reflected and addressed in the diversity of paths. This variety is a blessing. In the world, if five people go to purchase a cloth, all have their own choice of color and style. Similarly, in the case of God-realization, if there were only one path, people whose *sanskārs* were different would not have been attracted to it. The variety of paths serves a wider spectrum of people with varying natures and *sanskārs*.

- *Swamiji*

## *Bhakti* is Essential for Success in Any Path

**Question:** One question has been haunting my mind, and I have already discussed it with my fellow-aspirants, but I am still looking for a satisfactory answer only from you. Many times Maharajji says in his discourses that even the *Karmī* and *Gyānī* cannot attain God without pursuing *Bhakti*. Why?

- *Shirish Sagathia, Ahmedabad, Gujarat*

**Answer:** Dear Shirish, God is Divine, while our instruments of *sādhanā*—the senses, mind, and intellect—are material. Whatever path we may follow, by our own *sādhanā*, we can never reach the Supreme Lord. But when God bestows His Grace, by His Divine energy He makes our senses, mind, and intellect Divine. And then we are able to see Him, hear Him, know Him, realize Him, and attain Him.

Thus, it is only by God's Grace that He is attained. This Grace of God requires that we please Him through *Bhakti*. Hence, the *Karmī* and *Gyanī* also need to do *Bhakti* for success in their *sādhanā*.

Alongside with *Bhakti*, you may keep any other *sādhanā*. If you do *Karm* and *Bhakti*, it will become *Karm Yog*; if you do *Gyān* and *Bhakti*, it will become *Gyān* Yog; and *Bhakti* by itself is *Bhakti Yog*, but without *Bhakti* no *sādhanā* will result in God-realization. Our link with God will be established through *Bhakti* alone.

- *Swamiji*

## *Kuṇḍalinī*

**Question:** What is "*Kuṇḍalinī*," how is it awakened, and what are the benefits of awakening it?

- *Rajesh Kumar Tiwari, Yamuna Vihar, Delhi*

**Answer:** Dear Rajesh, The material energy, Maya, has

innumerable astounding powers and secrets within it. The inventions of the modern day world are only the tip of the iceberg of what exists within the womb of Mother Nature. The human body, which is made from Maya, also has many secrets and hidden potentials latent in it. Amongst these is the *Kuṇḍalinī*.

*Kuṇḍalinī* is a power that lies dormant at the base of the spinal column. Those who practice the *sādhanā* of *Haṭha Yog*, endeavor to awaken it by various means, and make it rise upwards through the spine. As the power ascends through the various *chakras* (circular regions) in the spine, it results in many *siddhis* (mystic abilities).

However, we must bear in mind that the *Kuṇḍalinī* is a material power, and not a spiritual power. The mystic abilities attained through it are purely material. If one's *Kuṇḍalinī* is awakened, it does not mean that the person has come closer to God, or has established a relationship with God. Also, if the *Kuṇḍalinī* is awakened without spiritual maturity, it leads to pride, which obstructs the spiritual progress of person. The *Kuṇḍalinī* is an immense power, and if it is not controlled properly, it can result in very deleterious side-effects. Very often, people who awaken it without sufficient bodily and mental preparation are unable to handle it, and suffer serious consequences. In some cases, the body gets ruined, and in other cases, the mind.

It is far safer not to go in that direction, and instead, strive to establish one's connection with God through devotion. Then by the Grace of the Lord, if we get any *siddhis*, we will also receive the power to protect ourselves from their pitfalls. The important thing is not the awakening of the *Kuṇḍalinī*, but the development of an intense longing for God.

## Meditating on *Chakras*

**Question:** Respected Swamiji, How does meditating on the *Anāhat chakra* help in God-realization? I have been practicing this for many months, because that was so natural to me.

- *Matthew Lehman, Raleigh, North Carolina*

**Answer:** Dear Matthew, There are seven main *chakras* in the body, along the spinal column. Meditating upon them leads to *siddhis*, or mystic powers, and also induces the upward movement of the *Kuṇḍalinī* power. *Chakra* meditation is recommended for people who have less faith in God, and have not yet understood the concept of the relationship of the soul with the Almighty.

This *chakra* meditation does not develop our love for God, or help us realize our eternal position as His servant. Hence, those who have faith in God, and have understood from the scriptures that we have an eternal relationship with Him, should not go for *chakra* meditation. Instead, they should try to meditate upon God, and His Names, Forms, Virtues, Pastimes, Abodes, and Saints.

- *Swamiji*

## Does Hinduism Mention the Caste System?

**Question:** Being born in a Hindu family and growing up in USA as an ABCD—American Born Confused Desi—has been very distressful. My intellect is riddled with questions, both—about the culture I was born in and the one I grew up in. One point that all my Western friends ask about Hinduism is regarding the caste system. Why is the caste system in the Vedas?

- *Robin Sharma, Portland, Oregon*

**Answer:** Dear Robin, The Vedas define duties at two levels:

1. Spiritual duties. These are our duties towards God, Who is our eternal Father, Mother, Friend, and Well-wisher. Performing these is called *Bhakti*, or devotion, and it results in the purification of the mind and the attainment of God. The spiritual duties, or *Bhakti*, are the eternal principles that always remain the same. They are also called *Par Dharm*, or the spiritual aspect of religion.

2. Social duties. When we think of ourselves to be the body, we have duties towards our parents, friends and relatives, the society we live in, the nation of which we are citizens, etc. These do not result in God-realization. However, fulfilling these duties ensures that we act in a socially responsible manner,

and contribute towards the well-being and harmony of society. These duties have been described in the Vedas, and are also called *Karm* or *Karm Dharm*. They are also called *Varṇāśhram Dharm*.

In this *Varṇāśhram* system, the duties were defined according to a person's nature and occupation. However, with the passage of time, the system got degraded and the classifications became based on birth. This social practice was a wrong interpretation of what was mentioned in the Vedas. But when the British ruled India, they highlighted the social practice, and called it the "caste system". They publicized it so much that even today in USA, if the discussion of Hinduism comes up, the only thing many people know about it is the caste system. They are not aware of the sublime knowledge of the science of God-realization that exists in Hinduism, which has no comparison anywhere in the world.

Interestingly, while living in India, very rarely do I come across any mention of castes. Everyone has forgotten about them. But when I come to USA, Hinduism is considered synonymous with the caste system.

It is thus necessary to clarify that the *Varṇāśhram* system was not a part of the spiritual principles of Hinduism. It was a set of social duties described in Hinduism thousands of years ago, when civilization in the western world had not even begun. Secondly, if it got distorted with time, that was a social defect, and Hinduism cannot be blamed for it. This is just as slavery existed in the western world until two hundred years ago, but we do not blame Christianity, Islam, or Judaism for this social practice. In fact, even until the 1960s, discrimination on the basis of skin color existed in USA. This was a social ill but we do not hold Christianity responsible for it. Similarly, the *Varṇāśhram* system got distorted as a social ill in India, but it is wrong to blame Hinduism for it.

- *Swamiji*

## Duty to Others versus Duty to God

**Question:** I have some question regarding duty. If someone becomes a *Karm Sanyāsī* (renounces the world), isn't that person forfeiting the duty to the parents? Isn't that a sin before the True path?

*- Bhikari Charan Sahu, Cuttack, Odisha*

**Answer:** Dear Bhikari Charan, We do have duties towards the biological parents. But God is our spiritual Father and Mother. We have a duty towards Him as well, and that duty is even more important than the worldly duties.

In the answer to the previous question, it has been explained that we have social duties towards society and spiritual duties towards God. If one gives up social duties due to irresponsibility, laziness, frivolity, etc., it is definitely a sin; but if one renounces the social duties to embrace spiritual duties, it is not considered a sin. When we surrender to God, we are automatically taking care of all duties, just as when we water the root of a tree, the water automatically reaches all the branches, fruits, and flowers of the tree.

Even in the world, if someone joins the army to discharge his duty to the nation, he is forsaking his duty to his parents. He could be killed on the battlefield, leaving the old parents without a support. But his joining the army is not considered dishonorable; rather it is an act of bravery. This is because that person is giving up a lower duty to take up a higher one. Similarly, the *Karm sanyāsī* does forsake the worldly duties to parents etc., but he accepts the higher duty towards God, and so he is not committing a sin.

However, the path of *Karm sanyās* should only be chosen under the guidance of a Guru. For the majority of the people, the path of *Karm Yog* is more suitable. This has been described in the chapter on *Karm Yog*.

*- Swamiji*

## Vedic View of other Religions

**Question:** Is Islam basically a defective religion? Is there any way to judge which religion is a true religion, and which is not?

*- Sudhakar Rao, Serangoon, Singapore*

**Answer:** Dear Sudhakar, First let me clarify that there is only one person who has the right to pass judgments on such grave matters, and that is God Himself. Our judgments are often based on inadequate data and understanding.

All the Prophets in history delivered their message in accordance with the time, place, and circumstance in which they were preaching. Without understanding this principle, we could jump to rash judgments on their teachings. The Hindu scriptures declare that the Buddha was God Himself. And yet He preached a religion that accepts neither the concept of God nor the soul. The emphasis is only on cleansing your mind.

सच्चित्त परियोदपनं एतं बुद्धानुशासनम्। (धम्मपद)

*sachchitta pariyodapanaṁ etaṁ buddhānuśhāsanam*

*(Dhammapad)*

The *Dhammapad* states that the essence of all teaching is to cleanse the mind. The reason is that at the time of Gautam Buddha, people were over-indulging in the ritualistic aspect of the Vedas. They were engaging in animal sacrifice. Hence, the Buddha preached a philosophy that helped people rise from the platform they were at. Buddhism was the perfect philosophy for the people in that situation and at that time. Now, if we were to say that Buddhism is a bad religion because it does not mention the existence of God, how far from the truth we would be.

Similarly, Christianity too may seem elementary in comparison to the Vedic philosophy, yet it lifted society up from barbarism two millennium years ago, and has served humankind since then. If we read the writings of Thomas Kempis, St. John of the Cross, and St. Francis of Assisi, we perceive their fervor for devotion and intoxication for God.

The same holds true for many Sufi saints, like Maulana Jalaluddin Rumi, Nizamuddin Aulia, Amir Khusroo, and Moinuddin Chisti. When I was a child, there was a five-year old Hindu girl in the neighborhood who used to read the Namaz, without ever having learnt it from anyone (she forgot it by her sixth year). It is possible that she was a good Muslim in her previous life, and God arranged for her to continue the journey by giving her an appropriate Hindu birth in this life.

So God alone is aware of the full importance of any religion in the development of humankind, and its impact on the development of culture, architecture, literature, music, etc. A religion carries an entire civilization on its back for ages and ages. How then can we reject any religion as bad?

Very often religious practitioners develop intense enmity with each other on the basis of the God they worship. The Vedic scriptures give us a broader vision. They clearly state:

एकं सत विप्रः बहुधा वदन्ति। (ऋग्वेद १.१६४.४६)

*ekaṁ sata viprah bahudhā vadanti (Ṛig Ved 1.164.46)*

"The Absolute Truth is one, but devotees call Him by many names." The Creator of the world is one. All the religions are worshiping the same all-powerful God. Quarrels are due to lack of understanding. This is like the story of some blind people who went to see an elephant. One of them put his hand on the elephant's stomach and exclaimed, "This creature is just like a wall."

The second man caught the leg of the elephant and stated, "This animal is like a tree."

The third caught the tail and said, "The elephant is like a rope."

The fourth caught the elephant's ear and said, "It is like a fan." Now they all started fighting.

One man with eyes was watching these blind men. He pacified them, "Do not fight. None of you is wrong. All of you are describing parts of the same elephant. All that you have said together makes the complete elephant."

Like the blind men who were fighting because they thought that the part they had caught was the entire elephant, the followers of different religions too fight because they think that the spiritual knowledge they possess is the ultimate. One says that if you believe in this personality, you will go the heaven; else you will go to hell. The other says that if you believe in that Saint, you will be saved; else you will be doomed for eternity.

The Vedas give us the view of the entire elephant, i.e. from the ABCD of spirituality till the subtlest Divine knowledge. The Vedic philosophy reveals the perennial principles of spirituality, irrespective of time, place, and circumstance. It was not created on a particular date in history, for fulfilling a particular need of society, rather is based on the Vedas, which are the eternal knowledge of God.

Hence, the religion mentioned in the Vedas is called *Sanātan Dharm*, or "Eternal Religion." This *Sanātan Dharm* has become known worldwide as Hinduism. Hence, Hinduism teaches us tolerance and respect for all devotees and religions, without in any way tarnishing the Supreme position of the Vedas.

- *Swamiji*

# 9

# *Karm Yog*

## The *Karm Yog* of the Bhagavad Geeta

**Question:** Namaste Swamiji! I'm working with a marketing firm. My dilemma is my job asks for too much of sales pressure and by the time I go home, I can't forget that. I am not able to do *sādhanā* because of it. My family has gone to spend one fortnight in Maharajji's *āśhram*, but I cannot go, and *nirāśhā* (disappointment) is covering me. Please help.

- *Shambhunath Dixit, Meerut, Uttar Pradesh*

**Answer:** Dear Shambhunath, There are two ways of remembering God and Guru. The first is to sit down and meditate on Them. The second is to work in the consciousness "I am doing this work for Their pleasure." The second way may be more difficult, but it takes us to a higher level of Divine Love. This is because it develops the spirit of *sevā*, or service.

Even though your present job may be burdensome, you can easily do the second kind of remembrance. Whatever you earn from your job, use a portion of it to serve the mission of your Spiritual Master. In this way, by offering the fruits of your work to God, you will develop the consciousness that you are working for His pleasure. You will then not look at your work as separate from your devotion, but as an integral part of it.

This is the *Karm Yog* of the Bhagavad Geeta:

यत्करोषि यदश्नासि यज्जुहोषि ददासि यत्।
यत्तपस्यसि कौन्तेय तत्कुरुष्व मदर्पणम्।। (भगवद् गीता ९.२७)

*yatkaroṣhi yadaśhnāsi yajjuhoṣhi dadāsi yat*
*yattapasyasi kaunteya tatkuruṣhva madarpaṇam*
*(Bhagavad Geeta 9.27)*

"Arjun! Whatever you do, whatever you eat, whatever austerities you perform, and whatever you give away, do it as an offering to Me."

Along with working in this spirit, whenever you find the time, you should also practice the first kind of remembrance. For some time in the day, do no other work; simply sit and think of God and Guru. This will help you eliminate worldly consciousness from your mind and strengthen your devotional sentiment. Also, definitely spend some days every year with your Gurudev as well.

You may be thinking that if you did not have to work at all, then you could have spent all your time in devotion. However, there are two kinds of *vairāgya*, or detachment. The first kind is when you find the world as troublesome, and want to run away from it. Shree Krishna calls this *rājasic* detachment (detachment in the mode of passion):

दुःखमित्येव यत्कर्म कायक्लेशभयात्त्यजेत्।
स कृत्वा राजसं त्यागं नैव त्यागं फलं लभेत्।। (गीता १८.८)

*duḥkhamityeva yatkarma kāyakleśhabhayāttyajet*
*sa kṛitvā rājasaṁ tyāgaṁ naiva tyāgam phalaṁ labhet*
*(Bhagavad Geeta 18.8)*

"Giving up one's work, thinking it to be burdensome and painful, is to be considered *rājasic* detachment; it does not lead to Divine fruits."

The second kind of detachment is where you continue working, while giving up attachment to the results. In other words, you practice equanimity in pain and pleasure, success and failure, hardship and luxury, favorable and unfavorable situations. Shree Krishna calls this *sāttvic* detachment (detachment in the mode of goodness):

कार्यमित्येव यत्कर्म नियतं क्रियतेऽर्जुन।
संगं त्यक्त्वा फलं चैव स त्यागः सात्त्विको मतः।।

*kāryamityeva yatkarma niyataṁ kriyate 'rjuna*
*saṅgaṁ tyaktvā phalaṁ chiava sa tyāgaḥ sāttviko mataḥ*
*(Bhagavad Geeta 18.9)*

"Performing one's work, simply because it is to be performed, while giving up attachment to the fruits, is *sāttvic* detachment."

Hence, the proper path for spiritual progress is to practice devotion along with our prescribed work, even though it may be painful and burdensome. When our detachment develops to such an extent that we no longer find our work burdensome, no matter how difficult it may be, only then should we consider giving up work, and performing devotion full-time. However, this step of Karm *Sanyās* is to be taken only under the guidance of the Guru, when we are qualified for it. For the vast majority of the people, *Karm Yog* is more suitable, where they continue doing their work, but make their consciousness Divine.

While doing *Karm Yog*, you can remember God and Guru in various ways. Practice to feel Their presence with you. Think that They are watching you; make Them your witness in every activity that you perform. This will help keep your mind in the Divine realm, while you do your worldly duties with the body.

*- Swamiji*

## Stress Management

**Question:** Whenever I am in *satsaṅg*, I feel de-stressed but once I am out of *satsaṅg*, the stress level increases. My question is how to get relieved of stress permanently?

*- Shiv Kumar Maheshwari, Patel Nagar, New Delhi*

**Answer:** Dear Shiv, We experience stress because we want certain outcomes, situations, and results. However, the soul is not independent, and it is not within its ability to fulfill all of its desires. By nature, the soul is a servant of God. Now, what is the duty of the servant? To fulfill the wishes of the master. If we surrender to God and think that whatever He does is for our welfare, this attitude of surrender will help us get rid of stress. A surrendered soul says:

राज़ी हैं उसी में जिसमें तेरी रज़ा है।
यूँ भी वाह वाह है त्यों भी वाह वाह है।।

*rāzī haiñ usī meñ jisameñ terī razā hai*
*yūñ bhī vāha vāha hai tyoñ bhī vāha vāha hai*

"I am happy in Your happiness. Whatever situation You put me in, I will blissfully accept it." Thus, stress is a symptom of lack of our submission to the Will of God. When we experience stress, the best medicine to cure it is to increase our level of surrender.

Now, what is the problem in increasing the level of surrender? Worldly attachments! We keep on pondering, "This should happen this way; that should happen that way." That is the main hurdle to complete surrender. For achieving that goal, we need to increase our detachment from the world.

Before God-realization, there will always be some amount of tension within everyone, because the extent of surrender will not be one-hundred percent. However, by giving us tension, God signals to us that something is wrong and we need to correct it by surrendering further to Him. This is just as when we put our hand in the fire, we feel pain. What would happen if we did not feel the pain? Our hand would burn without our knowing it. The feeling of pain is, in fact, a form of Grace. It is a signal that something is wrong, and that we must take the hand out. Similarly, stress is a signal that we need to increase our surrender and devotion to God.

A spiritual doctor will prescribe you the medicine of submitting to God for getting rid of stress, whereas a material doctor will give you all kinds of medicinal drugs. However, such drugs will not help eradicate the root cause of stress. By increasing the level of surrender, the source of stress will itself be eradicated. Shree Krishna states in the famous verse:

कर्मण्येवाधिकारस्ते मा फलेषु कदाचन।
मा कर्मफलहेतुर्भूर्मा ते संगोऽस्त्वकर्मणि।। (गीता २.४७)

*karmaṇyevādhikāraste mā phaleṣhu kadāchana*
*mā karmaphalaheturbhūrmā te saṅgo 'stvakarmaṇi*

*(Bhagavad Geeta 2.47)*

"Work with full dedication. Do not be careless while performing your tasks. But do not get attached to the fruits of those works." Shree Krishna again says:

योगिनः कर्म कुर्वन्ति संगं त्यक्त्वात्मशुद्धये।। (गीता ५.११)

*yoginaḥ karma kurvanti saṅgaṁ tyaktvātmaśhuddhaye*

*(Bhagavad Geeta 5.11)*

"A *yogī* is one who can work without any attachment to the results." If we follow this formula, stress will be abolished from its roots.

- *Swamiji*

## Working without Desires

**Question:** Today I was listening to your *Karm Yog* speech. You said, "Do your *Karm*, but do not desire." I am not able to understand how can you do *Karm* without desire? I think it's difficult to implement this in life. Let's take an example: if any student desires to become a doctor, he can start focusing on medical studies. If he doesn't desire, it will be difficult for him to achieve it. Then how can we work without desire?

- *Hari Dutta, Baripada, Mayur Bhanj, Odisha*

**Answer:** Dear Hari, Your question is in regard to *Karm Yog*. The principle of *Karm Yog* is to work without desire. But, you have asked that if we give up desire, how can we do any work at all. All work begins with a desire to achieve the results, and if there is no desire, there will be no work either.

The answer to this question is that desire is very basic to the nature of the soul, just as heat and light are basic to the nature of fire. A state of desirelessness is as impossible for the soul, as is the state without heat and light for the fire. Now, *Karm Yogīs* stop desiring for their own happiness, but that does not mean that they become desire less. They desire to love God, to please Him, and to attain Him. This spiritual desire to serve Him is the motivation behind all their actions.

Since their work is for the pleasure of God, they are not attached to its fruits. If after putting in their best efforts, they do not get their endeavored fruit, they remain undisturbed, for they accept it as the will of God. On the other hand, if their work was motivated by personal interests, if they do not get the desired result, they will get disturbed. So the acid test whether our desire is for the service of God or for self-gratification is our response to lack of success. If we are disturbed, it will mean that there was self-seeking in it; if we calmly accept it and continue working with enthusiasm, it is an indication that we wanted the fruits for the pleasure of God.

- *Swamiji*

**Question:** Being a Pediatric Doctor and entering into family life, I am not able to remember Guruji & God as I was doing before marriage. None of my family-members is co-operating for the same. Sometimes I think of leaving the family. Please guide me.

- *Krishnakant Sanghi, Indore, Madhya Pradesh*

**Answer:** Dear Krishnakant, Renouncing your profession and family to do *sādhanā* is the path of *Karm Sanyās*. Now, the life of a renunciant is not a cakewalk as it may seem from far. Many difficulties, obstacles, and issues need to be resolved there, just as in any worldly vocation. Today you find that along with practicing your profession and family life, you are unable to remember God and Guru, and you wish to take *Sanyās*. What if tomorrow you were to become a *Sanyāsī*, and then find that you are still not able to remember God and Guru? You would then neither be here nor there.

The Saint Tulsidas states:

ब्रह्म ज्ञान जान्यो नहीं कर्म दिये छिटकाय।
तुलसी ऐसी आत्मा सहज नरक महँ जाय।।

*brahma gyāna jānyo nahīñ karma diye chhiṭakāya*
*tulasī aisī ātmā sahaja naraka mahañ jāya*

"One who does not possess the required enlightenment for *Sanyās*, and yet prematurely renounces the worldly duties, goes downwards to hell." This is a path that should be taken only under the guidance of a Guru, who can judge your eligibility for it.

The Guru will, depending upon your *sanskārs*, first advise you to do devotion without changing your station in life. Practice living in the world without letting the world live in you. When you have reached the point where you are doing the maximum devotion and *sevā* possible, but you yearn to do even more, then the Guru may instruct you to leave the world. But again, for someone who has already entered family life, it may be socially too disrupting to leave the family, and the Guru may instruct you to continue with *Karm Yog*, until the children are settled.

There are so many inspiring examples of great *Bhakti* Saints who were *Karm Yogīs*, such as Kabir, Guru Nanak, Ekanath, Naamdev, Tukaram, Jayadev, etc. The Saint Kabir has put this very nicely:

सुमिरन की सुधि यों करो, ज्यौं सुरभि सुत माहिं।
कहे कबीर चारो चरत, बिसरत कबहुँक नाहीं॥

*sumirana kī sudhi yoñ karo, jyauñ surabhi suta māhiñ*
*kahe kabīra chāro charata, bisarata kabahuñka nāhīñ*

"Just as a cow grazes grass in the field all day, while constantly remembering its calf at home, you too remember your Lord while going about your daily duties." Many *Karm Yogīs* in ancient history, were great kings, such as, Ambarish, Dhruv, Prahlad, Prithu, Yudhishthir, etc. They were great kings, discharging their required duties and yet maintaining remembrance of God. The Bhagavad Geeta too is all about *Karm Yog*. Arjun wanted to leave his duties, thinking them to be burdensome, but Shree Krishna repeatedly instructed him:

सर्वेषु कालेषु मामनुस्मर युध्य च। (भगवद् गीता ८.७)

*sarveṣhu kāleṣhu māmanusmara yudhya cha*
*(Bhagavad Geeta 8.7)*

"Always think of Me, and also do your duty." Swami Vivekananda very aptly summarized this as follows: "Devotion can be practiced even in the battlefield; the Bhagavad Geeta was preached there."

It is only at the end that Shree Krishna said:

सर्वधर्मान्परित्यज्य मामेकं शरणं व्रज। (गीता १८.६६)

*sarvadharmānparityajya māmekāṁ śharaṇaṁ vraja*
*(Bhagavad Geeta 18.66)*

"Give up all duties, and surrender to Me alone." This instruction of *Karm Sanyās* has been given at the end. Thus, *Karm Sanyās* is also a bona fide path, but only for those rare few souls who have acquired the eligibility for it.

- *Swamiji*

# 10

# *Gyān* vs *Bhakti*

## Philosophic Viewpoints of *Āchāryas*

**Question:** Can you please explain, in Indian philosophy, what is the difference between *Advait vād*, *Dvait vād*, *Viśhiṣhṭ Advait vād*, *Dvait Advait vād*, *Viśhuddh Advait vād*, and *Achintya Bhedābhed vād*?

*- Peter Taylor, Stanford, California*

**Answer:** Dear Peter, These are names of the philosophies presented by the founders of various traditions in Hinduism. An important Vedic scripture is the *Vedānt Darśhan*; it is also called *Brahm Sūtra*. Many of the great *Āchāryas* (Spiritual Teachers) have written their commentaries on it. In these commentaries, the distinct philosophic stance they took to explain the relationship between God, the soul, and Maya, resulted in the name given to their philosophy.

Jagadguru Shankaracharya stated that there is only one entity in existence, called *Brahman* (or God). It has no form or attributes. The soul is not a separate entity from *Brahman*, rather the soul is *Brahman* itself, but covered by ignorance. The day that ignorance is dispelled, the soul will realize itself to be *Brahman*. He also stated that Maya does not exist; it is *mithyā* (an illusion) and we only perceive it due to ignorance. If our ignorance gets dispelled, Maya will cease to exist. Since Shankaracharya emphasized the existence of only one entity, his philosophy is called *Advait vād*, or Non-Dualism.

Jagadguru Ramanujacharya agreed that there is only one entity, *Brahman*, but stated that it possesses variety. Just as a tree is one but it has got branches, fruits, leaves, and flowers in it. Similarly, the *Jīva* (Soul) and Maya are *viśheṣhaṇ* (distinct attributes) of *Brahman*. Hence, he called his philosophy *Viśhiṣhṭ Advait vād,* or Qualified Non-dualism.

Jagadguru Madhvacharya took the opposite viewpoint. He emphasized five dualities:

1. Duality between one soul and another soul. This is evident by the fact that one soul gets liberated while the other is still bound, thus proving that all souls have their own distinct individuality.
2. Duality between the soul and Maya. Maya is insentient and non-conscious, while the soul is sentient and conscious.
3. Duality between Maya and Maya. We eat certain items and discard others as inedible, which proves that food items are different from each other. If they were all the same, we should not have hesitated in eating mud.
4. Duality between Maya and God. God is the All-powerful Creator. Maya is His energy. God is full of Divine Knowledge, Eternity, and Bliss. Maya is insentient and dependent upon God's power for its work.
5. Duality between the soul and God. The soul is under the bondage of Maya, while God is the governor of Maya and can never come under its sway; the soul is finite in its knowledge while God is all-knowing; the soul pervades its consciousness within one body while God pervades the entire universe; the soul is hankering for Bliss while God is an ocean of Bliss.

Since he emphasized dualities, his philosophy is called *Dvait vād*, or Dualism.

Jagadguru Nimbarkacharya said both, Non-dualism and Dualism, are right. A drop of water and the ocean can be called one, and they can also be called different from each other. Similarly, the soul is a part of God, so you can either club the soul and God together and call them as one entity, or you can distinguish them and say that they are distinct from each other. Hence, he propagated *Dvaitādvait vād*, or Dual Non-dualism.

Jagadguru Vallabhacharya propagated *Viśhuddh Advait vād*, or Pure Non-dualism. He stated that the Non-dualism of Shankaracharya is not correct, because he has denied the existence of Maya, and the existence of a distinct entity called the soul. The fact is that both—Maya and the soul—exist, but they are one with God. Hence, he called his philosophy *Viśhuddha-advait vād*, or Pure Non-dualism.

Chaitanya Mahaprabhu said that just as heat and light are the energies of fire, and they are simultaneously one and different from it, similarly, the soul and Maya are energies of God, and are simultaneously one and different from Him. He also added that both these concepts of difference and oneness cannot be fully comprehended by the intellect. Hence, he called his philosophy *Achintya Bhedābhed vād*, or Inconceivable Simultaneous Oneness and Difference.

These are the six major schools of Indian philosophy that have been accepted as authentic by the Vedic scholars. Each of these has further branches. For example, in *Advait vād*, there are many differing views: *Ajāt vād*, *Vivart vād*, *Avichchhed vād*, *Dṛiṣhṭi Sṛiṣhṭi* vād, *Sṛiṣhṭi Dṛiṣhṭi vād*, etc. Besides these, there are also other schools of Indian philosophy, which are less popular and less scholarly in the presentation of their philosophies.

*- Swamiji*

## Difference between *Gyān Yog* and *Bhakti Yog*

**Question:** Thank you Swamiji for writing this book, which we are eagerly awaiting to read. I would like to understand the difference between *Gyān Yog* and *Bhakti Yog*.

*- Phillip Douglas, Edmonton, Alberta, Canada*

**Answer:** Dear Phillip, You are most welcome. *Gyān Yog* is the path to God-realization based on the premise of *Advait vād*—that the soul itself is God; when it dispels its covering of ignorance and gets seated in knowledge, it will get liberated from the illusion of Maya. Then it will realize itself to be one with the formless *Brahman* for eternity, devoid of any form, attribute, activity, or qualities.

The *Gyān Yogī* strives to attain knowledge of the self, and be practically situated on that platform. This requires analyzing that one is not the body, senses, mind, intellect, and ego. First, this knowledge is understood theoretically, by hearing from the Guru and the scriptures. Then one repeatedly meditates on the knowledge and tries to realize it practically. In this manner, material desires related to the body diminish slowly. Finally, one gains practical insight into the nature of the self.

*Bhakti Yog* is based on the premise that the soul is an integral part of God; it has turned its back towards God, and hence it is suffering in the cycle of life and death because of Maya. This Maya is not an illusion; it is an energy of God. So the soul needs to surrender itself to God and attract His Grace, by which it will receive the Divine Knowledge, Love, and Bliss of God.

*Bhakti Yog* involves developing immense love for the Lord. In such a state, the devotee develops an intense longing to see God, meet Him, and be with Him. Whatever one does, the mind remains attached to God and the thoughts flow towards Him, like the rivers flow towards the ocean. Such love in the heart cleanses it of all impurities. With a pure heart, one begins to see God in all living beings and in all things. As the thoughts become sublime, the devotee experiences the unlimited Divine Bliss of God and becomes fully satisfied. On liberation, the soul does not become God; it goes to His Divine abode, and there in a Divine body, it eternally participates in the loving pastimes of God.

- *Swamiji*

## The Path of *Bhakti* is Easy

**Question:** Everyone says that *Bhakti Yog* is easy, while *Gyān Yog* is difficult. What is the reason for this?

*- Sandhya Rao, Vikas Puri, Delhi*

**Answer:** Dear Sandhya, understand this by comparing a baby kitten and a baby monkey. The kitten is tiny in size and delicate in build. Yet if it is to be moved from one place to another, it does not need to worry. Its mother holds the kitten with her mouth and carries it. On the other hand, in the case of the baby monkey, the onus is not taken by the mother. While she jumps from one branch of the tree to another, it is the baby monkey's responsibility to hold its mother tightly, else she will fall.

In the above analogy, the path of *Gyān Yog* is comparable to the monkey and its baby. It is based on self-effort. Since the premise is that the soul itself is the ultimate Supreme Entity, there is no concept of surrender to God or dependence upon His Grace. Hence, the aspirant strives on his or her own strength.

*Bhakti Yog* is comparable to the cat and its kitten. In *Bhakti Yog*, the aspirant learns to surrender to the Lord, and thus attracts His Grace. Through Grace, God assists and protects the devotee. Thus, the path of *Bhakti Yog* becomes easy compared to *Gyān Yog*.

In *Gyān Yog*, the danger of pride is enormous. The poor conditioned soul gets trapped in the ego of being God. In comparison, the path of *Bhakti* involves practicing humbleness before God, and hence the pitfall of pride becomes marginalized.

*- Swamiji*

**Question:** Why should we distinguish between *Gyān Yog* and *Bhakti Yog* as two different paths? Such divisions in the name of religion are the cause of so much of strife in the world, and the fighting between religions. There is only one entity called *Brahman* in existence, so why don't we stop making distinctions between different paths?

*- Neeraj Jajoria, USA*

**Answer:** Dear Neeraj, We must definitely try to see the wonderful form of God behind all things—sentient and non-sentient. Everything in creation has emanated from God; it is situated in God; and it is a manifestation of the energy of God. That is what both, *Bhakti* and *Gyān* teach us to do. Jagadguru Shree Kripaluji Maharaj expresses this sentiment repeatedly in his *kīrtans*:

चर अचर में लखहु अपनो, इष्ट कहँ नित प्यारे।

*chara achara meñ lakhahu apano, iṣhṭa kahañ nita pyāre*

"See the form of your *Iṣhṭa Dev* in all animate and inanimate entities." The lack of this vision of unity is what leads to animosity and hatred, and the senseless killings that have taken place in the religious wars in history. The perpetrators of such violence apparently have a world view, in which they see people not subscribing to their beliefs as enemies, who can be killed without compunction. Unpleasant divides in this world are created when we fail to see the connection between God and His creation.

However, this unity does not mean that we must neutralize all the diversities that exist. There is unity in diversity, and also diversity in the unity. That diversity is the expression of the greatness of God Himself, Who creates innumerable species of life, and innumerable varieties within each species.

Is it possible to live without seeing the diversity of creation? Imagine life without categories. Can we say that we hate categories, and so we do not distinguish between shirts and trousers? Can we wear them in place of each other, and when people laugh at our dress, tell them that we see this world as one, and so do not categorize kinds of clothes. Can a doctor tell the patient that he does not categorize, and so the patient should take any medicine from the cabinet? Such an interpretation of *Advait* would lead to insanity.

I am reminded of a story in this regard. A king was the disciple of a great Saint. He heard from the Saint that there is only one entity in this world, and that is God. The king found this philosophy very convenient. He began making love with the maidservants in the palace. This was brought to the notice of the queen, who asked her husband for an explanation to his characterless behavior.

The king replied, "My Spiritual Master has taught me the philosophy of *Advait vād*, or Non-dualism, which states that there is only one entity in existence. So now I have become a *Brahm gyānī*, and I do not see any distinction between my wife and other women."

The queen was very annoyed. She accosted the king's Guru, and asked him, "What philosophy have you taught my husband? He has begun engaging in adultery." The Saint was amused at the interpretation of *Advait* by his disciple. He taught a rejoinder to the queen.

When it was time for lunch, the queen put feces on a plate and served it to the king. He exclaimed, "What is this you have brought?"

"O King! This is a tasty delicacy."

The king retorted, "What rubbish! This is stool."

The queen said, "Dear husband. It seems that you are able to perceive the difference between stool and delicacies! But you were saying there is no variety in this world, and all is one."

Without accepting the diversity of life, it is not possible to live. If we express our distaste for categorization between *Gyān* and *Bhakti*, we have in effect created a distinction between categorized and non-categorized. If there is abhorrence for categories, then why see the difference between categorized and non-categorized? Why find the need to criticize categorization?

People in developed countries commonly use GPS navigators. This means they distinguish between different roads, else they could have thought them all as one, and taken any road that caught their fancy.

Similarly, there are various paths leading to the goal of life. All these paths are manifestations of the infinite variety created by God. We must definitely not harbor ill-feeling or ill-will towards anyone. However, we must clearly understand the pros and cons of each and then make an intelligent choice of the path we wish to follow.

*Gyān* and *Bhakti* are both praiseworthy, but it does not imply that there is no distinction between them. We must clearly understand the difference and the relationship between them. Then we will be in a position to reach our ultimate destination of God-realization.

- *Swamiji*

**Question:** In one of your lectures you said that without knowing God one cannot love Him, and again without loving Him one cannot know Him. Knowing is related to knowledge (*Gyān*) and loving is related to devotion (*Bhakti*). So which is more important for a seeker—*Gyān* or *Bhakti*?

- *Jayesh Patel, USA*

**Answer:** Dear Jayesh, The topic "*Gyān* vs *Bhakti*" is one of the most intensely debated topics in Indian philosophy, and followers of *Advait vād*, *Dvait vād*, *Viśhiṣhṭ Advait vād*, *Viśhuddh Advait vād*, *Dvait Advait vād*, *Achintya Bhedābhed vād*, all hold strong opinions on either side of the topic.

It is difficult to do justice to this topic in brief. *Gyān* and *Bhakti* are definitely interrelated. For example, if someone gives us a piece of jewelry, and we have no knowledge of its worth, we will have no love for it either. But if we come to know that the gold is 24 carats, and the diamond studded in it is worth a million dollars, we will immediately develop immense love for it. Similarly, as we get knowledge of the glory of God and our relationship with Him, our devotion towards Him will also increase. True knowledge definitely leads to *Bhakti*.

Conversely, as we engage in *Bhakti*, God seated within the heart will give us deeper and newer realizations. Thus, *Bhakti* leads to *Gyān*. They are both intimately interrelated: *Gyān* increases *Bhakti*, and *Bhakti* increases *Gyān*.

However, *Gyān Yog* is not the same as *Gyān*. It is a path of *sādhanā* based on a particular philosophic viewpoint. It suggests that the soul is itself God, and by situating oneself in the knowledge of the *ātman* (self), one will attain liberation. Consequently, the meditational styles of the *Gyān Yogī* and the *Bhakti Yogī* are quite different. The *Bhakti Yogī* meditates on the Supreme, All-powerful God, and relates to

Him in a personal form as his *Iṣhṭa Dev.* However, the *Gyān Yogī* considers meditation on God as inferior, and aims to still the mind by meditation on the breath, a void, or the eyebrow center, etc. Such meditations, aimed at stilling the mind, are not only exceedingly difficult, they are also bereft of God's Grace.

The mind is a product of the material energy, and it cannot be conquered without Divine Grace, no matter for how many ages we may endeavor. Hence, Sage Patanjali, has mentioned thrice in his brief treatise:

ईश्वरप्रणिधानात्। (योग दर्शन १.२३)

*īśhvarapraṇidhānāt (Yog Darśhana 1.23)*

"Success in meditation and conquest of the mind will come by surrendering to God." Thus, *Bhakti* is essential in the path of *Gyān Yog* as well.

There is yet another kind of knowledge, called *Śhābdik Gyān*, which means dry intellectual knowledge, without concomitant practice. Such *Gyān*, which is without realization, leads to pride, and does more harm than good. Thus, it has been criticized by the scriptures.

The knowledge of the *Gyān Yogī* is incomplete without the understanding that soul is only a tiny fragment of God, it has an eternal relationship with God, and that it needs to surrender to God to attain His grace. We must acquire the right knowledge of our eternal relationship with God, and then endeavor to put it in practice. That knowledge will then help us increase our devotion, and devotion will increase our knowledge, and knowledge will increase our devotion, and devotion will increase knowledge, and so on...

- *Swamiji*

**Question:** If the soul is a part of God, then why did a great Saint such as Jagadguru Shankaracharya say that the soul is God Himself? Did he not understand the scriptures?

- *Seshashayi Venkatraman, Chennai, Tamil Nadu*

**Answer:** Dear Seshashayi, When the *Nitya Siddha Mahāpuruṣhas*, or eternally liberated Saints descend upon this earth, they preach according to *Deśh*, *Kāl*, and *Pātra* (time, place, and circumstance). The teacher may be D.Litt. but if he is teaching Grade One students, he will explain simple Mathematics: five minus three is equal to two. It does not mean that the teacher only knows that much; it means that the students can only understand so much.

Even before Shankaracharya, came Gautam Buddha. He was an Avatar of Lord Vishnu, and hence He is respected and worshipped by Hindus. But while propagating His philosophy, He did not accept the authority of the Vedas. The reason for this has been explained in the previous chapter "Paths to God-realization" under the topic "Vedic view of other religions."

When Shankaracharya came on this earth, a few hundred years after the Buddha, Buddhism had spread all over *Bharatvarsh* (India). In accordance with its philosophy, people believed in voidism, or the non-existence of the soul and God. In that atheistic environment, it was not possible to preach the glories of devotion to Shree Ram and Shree Krishna. So Shankaracharya accomplished the task of bringing the people back to the Vedas. To do this, he emphasized the formless, attributeless, all-pervading *Brahman*. However for himself, he was a great devotee of the personal form of God, and wrote hundreds of verses in praise of the various Avatars.

The following conversation is from Shankaracharya's Praśhnāvalī.

One of his disciples asked:

मुमुक्षुणा किं त्वरितं विधेयम्?

*mumukṣhuṇā kiṁ tvaritaṁ vidheyam?*

"What should that soul, who earnestly desires salvation, do?"

Shankaracharya replied:

सत्संगतिर्निममतेशभक्तिः।

*satsaṅgatirnimamateśhabhaktiḥ*

"He should break the bonds of material attachment and engage in devotion to God."

Again, his disciple asked him:

किं कर्म कृत्वा न हि शोचनियम्?

*kiṁ karma kṛitvā na hi śhochaniyam?*

"What is that work which does not lead to repentance later?"

Shankaracharya immediately replied:

कामारि-कंसारि-समर्चनाख्यम्।

*kāmāri-kansāri-samarchanākhyam*

"Only one who engages in devotion to Shree Krishna has no regrets later."

In fact, Shankaracharya, the unrivaled propagator of *Advait vād*, advised his mother to practice *Bhakti*, and blessed her with a vision of Shree Krishna. Now, listen to his next proclamation:

काम्योपासनयार्थयन्त्यनुदिनं किंचित्फलं स्वेप्सितम्
केचित् स्वर्गमथापवर्गमपरे योगादियज्ञादिभिः।

*kāmyopāsanayārthantyanudinaṁ kiñchitphalaṁ svepsitam*
*kechit svargamathāpavargamapare yogādiyagyādibhiḥ*

अस्माकं यदुनन्दनांघ्रियुगलध्यानावधानार्थिनाम्
किं लोकेन दमेन किं नृपतिना स्वर्गापवर्गैश्च किम्।।(प्रबोधसुधाकर २५०)

*asmākaṁ yadunandanāṅghriyugaladhyānāvadhānārthinām*
*kiṁ lokena damena kiṁ nṛipatinā svargāpavargaiśhcha kim*
*(Prabodhasudhākara 250)*

"Those who perform the ritualistic activities described in the Vedas for the attainment of the heavenly planets, and those who engage in the *sādhanās* of *Gyān* and *Yog* for the attainment of impersonal liberation, are both unintelligent. They may do as they wish, but I desire neither heaven nor liberation. I only wish to drink the nectar emanating from the lotus feet of the Supremely Blissful form of Shree Krishna. I am a *Rasik* who is anxious for the Bliss of Divine Love."

- *Swamiji*

# 11

# The Personal Form of God

## Formless vs Personal Form of God

**Question:** God is formless and without limiting attributes of names, shapes, and qualities. So am I right in concluding that Krishna, Ram, Shiv, etc. cannot be God, for they possess a form?

- *Sebastian Diaz, San Diego, California*

**Answer:** Dear Sebastian, There is One Supreme God, and He is All-powerful. He has created this world around us, which is full of shapes and forms. If God can make a world with infinite forms, does He not have the ability to take on a form Himself? Definitely He does! If we say that He cannot have a form, then we do not accept Him as the All-powerful God. And if we admit that He is All-powerful, then we must also accept that He possesses the power to manifest a personal form for Himself.

At the same time, God is also formless. He exists everywhere in the world. For Him to be all-pervading, it is necessary that He should also be without a form.

God is perfect and complete, and so He is both—formless and possessing forms. We individual souls too have both aspects to our personality. The soul is formless, and yet, it has taken on a body; not once, but innumerable times in countless past lifetimes. If we tiny souls have the ability to take on a form, the All-powerful God can definitely take on a form whenever He wishes.

Hence, the Vedas state that there are both aspects to God's personality:

द्वे वाव ब्रह्मणो रूपे मूर्तं चैवामूर्तं च। (बृहदारण्यकोपनिषद् २.३.१)

*dve vāva brahmaṇo rūpe mūrtaṁ chaivāmūrtaṁ cha*

*(Bṛihadāraṇyakopaniṣhad 2.3.1)*

"God is formless and All-pervading, but He also manifests in a personal form." In the Vedic tradition, we are fortunate that we have descriptions of the personal forms of God, such as Shree Krishna, Shree Ram, Lord Shiv, Lord Vishnu, etc.

\- *Swamiji*

## The Sweetness of the Personal Form

**Question:** The Hari Bhakti Sudhodaya says: *brahmanāṇḍo bhavedeśh…* "The Bliss of the personal form of God is exceedingly sweeter than that of the formless *Brahm*." My mind cannot be convinced on this point. Please give some logic to persuade me of the same.

\- *Atmananada Mahapatra, Berhampur, Orissa*

**Answer:** Dear Atmananda, Consider an example to understand this point. Let us say that a woman is carrying a baby in her womb. Although she has not seen her baby as yet, she is happy at the thought that soon she will become a mother. After a few months, the baby is born and starts growing up. The mother holds her two year-old baby in her lap with great love. Now, ask that mother, "The joy you are experiencing from your baby, is it the same as the joy you got when the baby was in your womb."

The mother will say, "What are you saying? That was nine months of pain. This is real bliss. I can see my little daughter, hug her, hear her childish prattle, see her innocent pastimes, and serve her. When she was in the womb, it was just a feeling that I have a baby."

Similarly, those who worship the formless *Brahm*, cannot see their Lord; they cannot witness His sweet *Leelas*; they cannot hear the enchanting sound of His flute, or feel the love of His embrace. They can only experience Him in their minds. But worshipers of God in His form as *Bhagavān* are able to see the Divine form of Their Beloved Lord, participate in His sweet pastimes, and serve Him to their heart's content. They experience all the sweetness of the Names, Forms, Qualities, Pastimes, Abodes, and associates of God.

Hence, the highest Bliss of God is attained from His personal form as *Bhagavān*. This is called *Premānand*, or Divine Love Bliss. It is innumerable times sweeter than *Brahmānand*, the Bliss of the formless *Brahm*. They are both sweet, but one is sweeter. This is just as jaggery, sugar, and candy are all sweet, but if you were eating jaggery and someone put candy in front, you would leave the jaggery and pick up the candy. The jaggery is sweet, but sugar is sweeter, and candy is the sweetest.

- *Swamiji*

## The Advantages of Devotion to the Personal Form

**Question:** Dear Swamiji, Thank you for inviting questions via the Google group. I have a question for you. Why does the Bhagavad Geeta say that worshiping the Formless is very difficult for the embodied soul?

- *Manohar Joshi, Richardson, Texas*

**Answer:** Dear Manohar, Since eternity, we have been habituated to interacting with people and things possessing forms, shapes, attributes, etc. So our mind is naturally accustomed to forms. If we engage in meditation on the formless *Brahm*, it goes against our nature.

If you were asked to observe a light for six hours and contemplate on it, you would probably not be able to do so. Instead, if you were asked to see a wonderful drama, with a great story, attractive actors, and lots of action, you would thoroughly enjoy it and easily sit through the entire session.

Similarly, Shree Krishna says:

क्लेशोऽधिकतरस्तेषामव्यक्तासक्त चेतसाम्।
अव्यक्ता हि गतिर्दुःखं देहवद्भिरवाप्यते।। (भगवद् गीता १२.५)

*kleśho 'dhikatarasteṣhāmavyaktāsakta chetasām*
*avyaktā hi gatirduḥkhaṁ dehavadbhiravāpyate*

*(Bhagavad Geeta 12.5)*

"For the embodied soul it is very difficult to meditate on the unembodied *Brahm*; the path of worshipping the formless *Brahm* is full of difficulties."

Also, in the previous answer, it has been explained that the Bliss of the Personal Form of God is exceedingly sweeter than the Bliss of the Formless *Brahm*. Since our mind is drawn towards sweetness, it is easily attracted to the sweetness of the Personal form of God. This is called *Premānand*. In this, we can also take advantage of all the nectarine descriptions of the loving *leelas* of God, which have been described in the scriptures, for turning our mind towards Him.

\- *Swamiji*

## Many Gods in Hinduism

**Question:** In Hinduism, we have many Gods—Krishna, Ram, Shiv, Vishnu, Durga, etc. Are they all different Gods? And if so, are some of them bigger than the others?

\- *Ramesh Patel, Milpitas, California*

**Answer:** Dear Ramesh, The answer to your question is that these are not different Gods; They are different forms of the same Supreme Lord.

We too have many personalities. When a man goes to office, he is dressed formally. When he takes a walk in the park, he is dressed semi-formally. And when he is at home, he is dressed very informally. His wife does not become confused, thinking, "I had married one man. How come I have three husbands?" She knows very well that these are three different appearances of her one husband. Similarly, Krishna, Ram, Shiv, Vishnu, etc. are all different forms of the same one God. We should not consider any one of these as bigger or smaller than the others. This is stated in the Vedas:

एकं संतम् बहुधाय कल्पयन्ति। (ऋग्वेद १०-११४.५)

*ekaṁ santam bahudhāya kalpayanti (Ṛig Veda 10-114.5)*

"The Absolute Truth is one but it has been described in a variety of ways by the Saints."

While comparing the example of a worldly person with God, we must also note the difference. A worldly person is not all-powerful; he cannot exist in all three places at the same time. However, God is supremely powerful. He can manifest in as many forms as He wishes and exist in all of them simultaneously. Hence, He eternally exists in the forms of Krishna, Ram, Shiv, Vishnu, etc. The true devotee respects all these forms of God, although doing devotion to any one of Them.

\- *Swamiji*

## Choosing One's *Iṣhṭa Dev*

**Question:** There was a Ram temple in our house; I was in the habit of hearing the Tulsi Ramayan, and meditating on the form of Lord Ram. But after marriage, in my in-laws' house, I began reading the Durga *Saptaśhati* and observing *Navrātras*. When I heard the *Bhāgavat saptāh*, I liked the *leelas* of Shree Krishna. How should I decide which God to worship?

\- *Savitri Bharani, Indore, Madhya Pradesh*

**Answer:** Dear Savitri, Although Ram, Durga, Krishna are all different forms of the one Supreme Lord, yet it is advisable to focus your devotion on a single form. There is a Hindi saying:

एक साधे सब सधे, सब साधे सब जाय।

*eka sādhe saba sadhe, saba sādhe saba jāya*

"If you focus all your attention on a single activity, you will succeed in it. But if you try to succeed in multifarious things at the same time, you will fail in all of them." With the same logic, if you try to love all the forms of God, you will end up loving none. But if you devote your mind to one form, you will develop love for all of them. So you must choose one form to worship, which is called "*Iṣhṭa Dev*", or the devotee's chosen form of God for devotion.

Now the question you have asked is about how to choose your *Iṣhṭa Dev*. In deciding this, you must consider which form of God is attractive to the mind. If your *Iṣhṭa Dev* has a beautiful form, you will find it much easier to meditate on Him. Also, if your *Iṣhṭa Dev* has wonderful pastimes, it will be very helpful in your devotion. To turn your mind towards God, *leelas* also play an important role. By hearing and chanting those *leelas*, devotees increase their love for God. From both these view points, devotion to Shree Ram and Shree Krishna is both—sweet and easy. Hence, They are also the most popular *Iṣhṭa Devs* in India. Their sweet pastimes are lovingly sung and remembered in temples and houses in every part of the country.

Amongst Them, Shree Krishna manifests four special nectars, above and beyond any other Avatar of God:

1. Exceptionally attractive form (His famous three-fold bending form with a flute on His lips).
2. Amazing sweetness of His flute that attracts even Lord Shankar.
3. The sweetest childhood pastimes that enchant the minds of devotees.
4. *Leelas* displaying the greatness of love, which reveal how God forgets His Almightiness because of the love of his devotees.

For all these reasons, I would highly recommend that you make Shree Krishna and His Divine Consort, Shree Radha Rani, as your *Iṣhṭa Dev*. However, if you decide to choose any other form of God, that is also fine.

*- Swamiji*

## Shree Ram vs Shree Krishna

**Question:** In Bhagavad Geeta Lord Krishna said: "*sarva dharmān parityajya mām ekaṁ śharaṇaṁ vraja*." If a person is a devotee of Ram, does that person have to surrender to Krishna and leave Lord Ram?

*- Sandeep Sethi, Penang, Malaysia*

**Answer:** Dear Sandeep, When Shree Krishna said, "Give up all varieties of religiosity and surrender to Me," He meant "Surrender to God." If you surrender to Supreme Almighty in any of His forms, you will be obeying the instructions of the Bhagavad Geeta. So you can continue worshiping Lord Ram, and yet fulfill Shree Krishna's instruction regarding complete surrender to His lotus feet.

- *Swamiji*

## Changing One's *Iṣhṭa Dev*

**Question:** Is changing of *Iṣhṭa Dev* allowed by *śhāstras*? What will happen if I am worshiping Lord Ram as my *Iṣhṭa Dev*, but switch to Lord Krishna?

- *Subir Chakraborty, Kolkata, West Bengal*

**Answer:** Dear Subir, With proper deliberation and understanding, for the purpose of spiritual progress, if you change your *Iṣhṭa Dev*, there is nothing wrong with it.

If Ram and Krishna had been different personalities, there would have been scope for concern. But when They are the same Supreme All-powerful Lord, then where is any ground for fear? In fact, all the eternal associates of Shree Ram came again during the descension of Shree Krishna.

- Lakshman came as Balaram
- Bharat came as Pradyumna (Shree Krishna's son)
- Shatrughna came as Aniruddha (Shree Krishna's grandson in Dwarika)
- Hanuman came too and sat on the flag of Arjun's chariot
- Soorpanakha came as Kubja
- Jambavant came in the same form and engaged in friendly combat with Shree Krishna

If there was the concern of changing one's *Iṣhṭa Dev*, then why would these eternal associates of Lord Ram descend to participate in the *leelas* of Shree Krishna? This shows that the fear of changing *Iṣhṭa Devs* exists only in our minds, and has no basis.

*- Swamiji*

## Problem of Many Deities in the Temple

**Question:** At present I want to know what to do with all the photographs or images of God various people have given me over the past thirty years. I seem to have a big collection because I have not figured out what to do with them. Please let me know what I can do with the photos/images.

*- Savita Khambampatti, Cincinati, Ohio*

**Answers:** Dear Savita, It is common to see many photos and images of various Gods in the houses of Indians. This may be acceptable in the first stage of devotion, but keeping so many images and photos reduces the focus on any one of them. As one gains more knowledge of God, and wishes to practice devotion more seriously, one should decide on an *Iṣhṭa Dev* to focus upon. The question of choosing one's *Iṣhṭa Dev* has been explained in a preceding question in this chapter. Once this step has been taken, then the question arises that you have asked. What to do with all the other images and photos?

There are two options. The first is to leave them in the temple as before, but worship only the image or photo of your *Iṣhṭa Dev.* The second option is bolder but more simplifying. Remove the images of the other forms of God from your altar at home. If you decide on the second option, you can go and give those images and photos to a temple. It is not difficult to find temples that will take and keep those images. Or you can immerse them midstream of a river, or in the ocean. That is the scripturally recommended way of disposing them.

People are often scared of this step, doubting if it would be considered an offence to simplify their temple in this manner, by reducing the number of images. However, God will never feel offended if we take this step to facilitate our devotion. Whether something is an offence or not is decided by intention with which we perform the action. If we do it out of laziness, or ill-will towards any of the forms of God, it may be considered a transgression. But if we take this step with the sincere intention of improving the focus of our devotion, God will be pleased rather than annoyed.

- *Swamiji*

## The Celestial Gods

**Question:** What about the celestial *devatās* such as *Indra*, *Varuṇ*, *Kuber*, *Agni*, *Vāyu*, etc.? What is their status in comparison to the Supreme God?

- *Aniruddha Sarkar, Pearland, Houston, Texas*

**Answer:** Dear Aniruddha, These *devatās* live in the higher planes of existence within this material world, called *swarg*. The *devatās* are not God; they are souls like all of us. They occupy specific posts in the administration of the world.

Consider the Federal government of a country. There is a Secretary of State, Finance Secretary, Industries Secretary, Agriculture Secretary, and so on. These are posts, and chosen people occupy those posts for a limited tenure. At the end of the tenure, the government changes, and all the post-holders change too. The posts of Secretary of State etc. do not cease to exist, but the persons holding the posts change.

Similarly, in the governance of the world, there are posts such as *Agni Dev* (the god of fire), *Vāyu Dev* (the god of the wind), *Varuṇ Dev* (the god of the ocean), *Indra Dev* (the king of the celestial gods), etc. Souls selected by virtue of their deeds in past lives occupy these seats for a certain amount of time. Then they are removed from their positions and others occupy these seats. Hence, souls get these posts of *Agni Dev*, *Vāyu Dev*, *Indra Dev*, *Varuṇ Dev*, etc. only temporarily. We cannot compare them to the Supreme Lord, Who is the All-powerful, Eternal, Creator, Maintainer, and Annihilator of the world. This distinction should be borne in mind between the various forms of God, and the celestial gods.

Many people worship the celestial gods for material rewards. However, we must remember that these *devatās* cannot grant either liberation from material bondage or God-realization. Even if they do bestow material benefits, it is only by the powers they have received from God. Thus, Shree Krishna says in the Bhagavad Geeta that people who worship the celestial gods are less intelligent. Those who are situated in knowledge worship the Supreme Lord.

*- Swamiji*

## Various Categories of Personalities

**Question:** What is the difference between *svānśhas*, *vibhinnānśhas*, and *nitya siddha* personalities?

*- Ravi Chauhan, New Delhi*

**Answer:** Dear Ravi, *Svānśhas* are expansions of Shree Krishna who are non-different from Him. They are all governors of *Yogmāyā*, such as Narayan, Ram, Shiv, etc. In other words, They are all God.

*Vibhinnānśhas* are fragments of the *Jīva Śhakti* of Shree Krishna. They can never be governors of *Yogmāyā*. If they turn their backs towards God, they are overpowered by the illusory energy, Maya. If they surrender to God, they are released from Maya forever, and thenceforth, they are governed by *Yogmāyā*.

*Nitya siddhas* are those souls who never had their backs towards God. They have eternally been with Him, participating in His Divine Pastimes in His Divine Abode. But they are under the sway of *Yogmāyā*, and not controllers of it.

*- Swamiji*

# 12

# Radha Rani

## *Yogmāyā*, the Divine Power of God

**Question:** I am not clear about the difference between Maya and *Yogmāyā*. Some people say that Mother Durga is the personification of *Yogmāyā*. Is this correct, and what is *Yogmāyā*?

*- Bimala Prasad Pattanayak, Athagarh, Odisha*

**Answer:** Dear Bimala, Maya is the external energy of God, with which He makes this material world. It is insentient, and all the gross and subtle objects in this world are made from Maya. *Yogmāyā* is the personal power of God, with which He governs all His other powers. It is through this *Yogmāyā* that He manifests His Divine abode, descends as an Avatar in the world, and displays His Divine pastimes. Through this power, He sits in the hearts of all the souls, notes their karmas and yet remains hidden from them. It is also by *Yogmāyā*, that God's Blissfulness, the sweetness of His Form, the sweetness of His flute, and the nectar of His virtues and pastimes are manifest. Most importantly for us, by virtue of *Yogmāyā*, God bestows Grace upon the souls of the world, granting them God-realization and Divine Love Bliss.

This *Yogmāyā* energy governs Maya, and then the material world is created. Hence, *Yogmāyā* is called the Divine Mother of the universe. This Divine power also manifests in the personal form as Durga, Seeta, Kali, Radha, Lakshmi, Mangala, Parvati, etc. So it is important to understand that these Personal Forms, Whom we see in pictures depicted sitting by the side of God, are not ordinary women. They are different personal forms of *Yogmāyā*.

*- Swamiji*

## Who is Radha?

**Questions:** What is the difference between Mother Durga and Radha Rani? My understanding is that by Mother Durga's mercy our sufferings can be mitigated, as She is the kind Mother of the world.

*- T. Dhanalakshmi, Auroville, Pondicherry*

**Answer:** Dear Dhanalakshmi, Radha and Durga are both the Divine *Yogmāyā* power of God. They are non-different from each other. Yet, there is a difference in the Bliss of Divine Love that we receive from both of Them.

This difference between Radha and Durga can be understood from the following story. One boy was coming home from school. On the way he was thinking that his mother will be at home; she will give him a loving hug; she will ask him about his day at school; she will have prepared tasty snacks for him; he will ask her to take him to the ice cream shop, and so on. However, when he reached home, he found a totally different scenario. His mother had a stick in her hand and was beating his elder brother.

The boy thought, "My mother's mood is not good at present. Let me quietly sneak away to my bedroom. When she is in a better mood, I will speak to her." The mother is the same, but one is her fierce form and the other is her loving form.

Similarly, Mother Durga is the form of *Yogmāyā* where She is combating and subduing demons. She is also engaged in administering the material energy, Maya, but Radha Rani is not concerned with any of these. She simply engages in the Loving Service of Shree Krishna and engages the souls in the same. She bestows the highest level of

Selfless Divine Love on the souls, and it is by Her Grace that one attains Shree Krishna. Those who know this secret and wish to relish the sweetness of Divine Love, worship the Divine Mother in Her sweetest form as Shree Radha.

*- Swamiji*

## Mention of Radha Rani in the Scriptures

**Question:** I have heard in the *Pravachans* (discourses) of many saints where they say that no description of Radha Rani exists in the Bhagavatam written by Maharishi Ved Vyas. I want to know whether there is any scriptural mention of Radha Rani. Or is it only a personal opinion?

*- Pragya Yadav, Patparganj, Delhi*

**Answer:** Dear Pragya, Your question addresses a widespread misnomer in the minds of many people. The nature of your question and its importance demands that detailed evidence be given from the scriptures for the benefit of everyone.

We shall come to the Shreemad Bhagavatam later. First of all, let us visit the other scriptures. Let us begin with the eternal Vedas, and see if they mention Radha Rani.

इदं ह्यन्वोजसा सुतं राधानां पते पिवा त्वस्य गिर्वणः। (ऋग्वेद ३.५१.१०)

*idaṁ hyanvojasā sutaṁ rādhānāṁ pate pivā tvasya girvaṇaḥ*

*(Ṛig Veda 3.51.10)*

"O Shree Krishna, Husband of Radha! Just as the *gopīs* worship You, the Veda *mantras* also worship You. By them, drink *Som Ras*."

विभक्तारं हवामहे वसोश्चित्रस्य राधसः सवितारं नृचक्षसम्।
(ऋग्वेद १.२२.७)

*vibhaktāraṁ havāmahe vasośchitrasya rādhasaḥ*
*savitāraṁ nṛichakṣasam (Ṛig Ved 1.22.7)*

"O All-knowing Witness seated in everyone's hearts, Who took Radha away from the *gopīs* (during the *Mahārās*)! We call You for our protection."

त्वं नृचक्सं वृषभानुपूर्वीः कृष्णास्वग्ने अरुषोविभाहि। (ऋग्वेद)

*tvaṁ nṛichaksaṁ vṛiṣhabhānupūrvīḥ kṛiṣhṇāsvagne aruṣhovibhāhi*
*(Ṛig Veda)*

In this *mantra*, the name of Vrishabhanu, father of Radha is mentioned, leaving no scope for doubt or interpretation on what the word "Radha" means.

यस्या रेणुं पादयोर्विश्वभर्ता धरते मूर्ध्नि प्रेमयुक्तः।
(अथर्व वेदीय राधिकोपनिषद्)

*yasyā reṇuṁ pādayorviśhvabhartā dharate mūrdhni premayuktaḥ*
*(Atharva Vedīya Rādhikopaniṣhad)*

"Radha is that Entity, the dust of Whose lotus feet, the Master of the Universe places on His head."

Next, let us come to the *Puraṇas*. Ved Vyas, who is the writer of the Shreemad Bhagavatam, has written seventeen other *Puraṇas* as well, and Radha Rani is mentioned in six of them.

यथा राधा प्रिया विष्णोः। (पद्म पुराण)
राधा वामांश संभूता महालक्ष्मीर्प्रकीर्तिता। (नारद पुराण)

*yathā rādhā priyā viṣhṇoḥ (Padma Purāṇa)*
*rādhā vāmānśha saṁbhūtā mahālakṣhmīrprakīrtitā*
*(Nārada Purāṇa)*

तत्रापि राधिका शश्वत्। (आदि पुराण)

*tatrāpi rādhikā śhaśhvat (Ādi Purāṇa)*

रुक्मिणी द्वारवत्यां तु राधा वृन्दावने वने।। (मत्स्य पुराण १३.३७)

*rukmiṇī dvāravatyāṁ tu rādhā vṛindāvane vane*
*(Matsya Purāṇa 13.37)*

राध्नोति सकलान् कामान् तेन राधा प्रकीर्तितः। (देवी भागवत पुराण)

*rādhnoti sakalān kāmān tena rādhā prakīrtitaḥ*
*(Devī Bhāgavata Purāṇa)*

आदौ राधां समुच्चार्य पश्चात्कृष्णं परात्परम्। (ब्रह्म वैवर्त पुराण)

*ādau rādhāṁ samuchchārya paśhchātkṛiṣhṇaṁ*
*parātparam (Brahm Vaivarta Purāṇa)*

Finally, let us come to the Shreemad Bhagavtam. This scripture was spoken by Shukadev Paramhans to Parikshit. Shukadev is an eternal associate of Radha Rani. He is a *Leela* Shuk, who takes the form of a parrot, and recites wonderful things in Her Divine abode, Golok. His love for Radha Rani is so much that if he takes Her Name, he faints for six months. Since, Parikshit was cursed to be bitten by a snake in seven days, Shukadev had to complete the Bhagavatam within that period, and so he did not take Radha Rani's name directly. But he made indirect mention of Her in many places. In the Radhopanishad, twenty-eight names of Radha Rani have been mentioned, including Gopi, Ramā, and Shree. Radha Rani is mentioned by some of these names in the Bhagavatam, for example:

कामयामह एतस्य श्रीमत्पादरजः श्रियः।
कुचकुंकुमगन्धाढ्यं मूर्ध्ना वोढुं गदाभृतः।। (श्रीमद् भागवतम्)

*kāmayāmaha etasya śhrīmatpādarajaḥ śhriyaḥ*
*kuchakuṅkumagandhāḍhyaṁ mūrdhnā voḍhuṁ*
*gadābhṛitaḥ (Shreemad Bhagavatam 10.83.42)*

"We want the dust of the lotus feet of Radha, whose *kuṅkum* is on the feet of Shree Krishna (because She placed His feet on Herself)." Here the word "Shree" has been used for Radha. If you say that "Shree" means Mahalakshmi, it is not applicable here because the Queens of Dwarika were themselves the descensions of Mahalakshmi. Why would they hanker for the dust of Mahalakshmi's lotus feet? The word "Shree" here refers to Radha.

रेमे रमेशो व्रजसुन्दरीभिर्यथार्भकः स्वप्रतिबिम्ब विभ्रमः।।
(श्रीमद् भागवतम् १०.३३.१६)

*reme rameśho vrajasundarībhiryathārbhakaḥ*
*svapratibimba vibhramaḥ (Bhāgavatam 10.33.16)*

"The Master of Ramā did *Rās* with the *gopīs*." Here the word "Ramā" has been used for Radha. Ramā can also mean Lakshmi, but that is not the usage here, since Vishnu, the Master of Lakshmi, does not do the *Rās leela*.

आक्षिप्तचित्ताः प्रमदा रमापतेस्तास्ता विचेष्टा जगृहुस्तदात्मिकाः।।
(श्रीमद् भागवतम् १०.३०.२)

*ākṣhiptachittāḥ pramadā ramāpatestāstā vicheṣhṭā*
*jagṛihustadātmikāḥ (Shreemad Bhagavatam 10.30.2)*

When Shree Krishna vanished during the *Mahārās*, the *gopīs* lamented and reached the state of *Mahābhāv*. They began imitating the pastimes of Ramāpati, the husband of Ramā. Again the word Ramā in the above verse, has come for Radha. It could not mean Lakshmi since Vishnu was not involved in this *leela*.

यां गोपीमनयत् कृष्णो (श्रीमद् भागवतम् १०.३०.३५)

*yāṁ gopīmanayat kṛiṣhṇo (Shreemad Bhagavatam 10.30.35)*

"Shree Krishna took one Gopi with Him and disappeared from the *Mahārās*." Gopi is also one of the names of Radha.

अनयाऽऽराधितो नूनं भगवान् हरिरीश्वरः। (श्रीमद् भागवतम्)

*anāyarādhito nūnaṁ bhagavān harirīśhvaraḥ*

*(Shreemad Bhagavatam 10.30.28)*

"This Gopi has performed great devotion to Shree Krishna. Hence He has taken Her alone with Him."

Apart from these, Radha is mentioned in many other scriptures. But in the context of this question, let these quotations suffice.

- *Swamiji*

## Krishna's Relationship with Radha

**Question:** Radha and Krishna were never married. Then what was the relationship between both of them?

- *Steve Martin, Baltimore, Maryland*

**Answer:** Dear Steve, Radha and Krishna are two aspects of the Supreme Personality. One is the Energetic and the other is the Divine Energy. The Upanishads state:

अनादिरयं पुरुषं एकमेवास्ति तदेव रूपं द्विधाविधाय
समाराधन तत्परोभूत् तस्मात्तां राधां रसिकानन्दां वेदविदो वदन्ति।
(साम रहस्योपनिषद्)

*anādirayaṁ puruṣhaṁ ekamevāsti tadeva rūpaṁ dvidhāvidhāya*
*samārādhana tatparobhūt tasmāttāṁ rādhāṁ rasikānandāṁ*
*vedavido vadanti (Sāma Rahasyopaniṣhad)*

"Since eternity, the one Supreme Lord has divided Himself in two forms, the Energetic and the Energy. That Supreme Energy (the *Yogmāyā* power) is Radha, Who is worshiped by the knowers of the Vedas."

Since Radha and Krishna are two aspects of the one Supreme Lord, They are inseparable from each other, just as milk and its whiteness are inseparable from each other, and fire and its light are one with each other. Thus, there is no question of separating Krishna and Radha.

However, in Their Divine pastimes, to relish the Bliss of Divine Love, They separate and again unite in many inconceivably sweet ways. These Divine pastimes of God are called *leelas*. When Shree Krishna and Radha Rani displayed Their *leelas* on the earth 5000 years ago, They relished the Bliss of *parkīya bhāv*, or love in the paramour sentiment. Thus, they were not married to each other. Nonetheless, the Garg Sanhitā describes Their *leelas* during another descension, where Radha and Krishna were married, and Brahma was the priest in the ceremony. In either case, Their *leelas* are Divine and beyond the social codes of conduct prescribed for us conditioned souls. Since They both are the same One Supreme Entity, the question of whether they married or not in the worldly sense, is not applicable.

*- Swamiji*

## Radha *Bhāv*, the Highest Ideal of Devotion

**Question:** The Gaudiya *sampradāya* glorifies "Radha *Bhāv*" as the highest devotional *Bhāv*. It is also mentioned in the writings of many of the *Bhakti* Saints. Can you please describe Radha *Bhāv* for me?

*- Sankirtan Dasa, Nabadwip, West Bengal*

**Answer:** Dear Sankirtan Dasa, Radha Rani, being the Divine power of Shree Krishna, has only one goal—selfless devotion towards Her Beloved. In fact, Divine Love is a subsidiary power of Radha Rani, and so the highest level of *Bhakti* resides in Her. This is characterized by intense longing for Shree Krishna, to the extent that is inconceivable to the human mind. The following verse gives a slight glimpse of this:

और्वस्तोमात्कटुरपि कथं दुर्बलेनोरसा मे,
तापः प्रौढो हरिविरहजः सह्यते तन्न जाने।
निष्क्रान्ता चेद्भवति हृदयाद्यस्य धूमच्छटापि,
ब्रह्माण्डानां सखिकुलमपिज्वालया जाज्वलीति॥

*aurvastomātkaṭurapi kathaṁ durbalenorasā me,*
*tāpaḥ prauḍho harivirahajaḥ sahyate tanna jāne*
*niṣhkrāntā chedbhavati hṛidayādyasya dhūmachchhaṭāpi,*
*brahmāṇḍānāṁ sakhikulamapijvālayā jājvalīti*

"When Radha does not have *darśhan* (sight) of Shree Krishna, the fire of the pain of separation in Her heart is so intense, that if the hazy lines above the smoke of that fire were to come out from Her body, the entire universe would burn to ashes." Such is the extent of Radha's longing for Shree Krishna.

Radha's devotion is also characterized by the highest level of selflessness, and complete absence of self-seeking. There is only one thought in Her mind—how to give happiness to Her Beloved. Such selfless devotion manifests in the *gopīs* to a lesser extent, and in other Saints to an even lesser extent. Thus, the topmost form of pure Divine Love resides in the heart of Radha. This is also called *Mādanākhya Mahābhav Bhakti.* All the other God-realized Saints, eternally liberated souls, and aspirants, derive inspiration from the nature of Radha's devotion. This devotion of Radha for Krishna has been termed as "Radha *Bhāv*" by poets and Saints.

- *Swamiji*

13

# Secret of God's Descension

## Faith in God's Divinity is Essential for *Sādhanā*

**Question:** The Bhagavad Geeta states that if we understand the secret of Shree Krishna's Divine birth and activities, we will not have to take birth in this material world again. This seems like overemphasis on understanding His birth and activities. But the Bhagavad Geeta cannot be wrong, since it is God's own word. Will you kindly explain how this can be true?

*- Pratap Kumar Swain, Cuttack, Odisha*

**Answer:** Dear Pratap, If we can perfect our devotion to God, we will not take birth in this material world again. But devotion is the process of making Divine sentiments towards God. Its foundation is faith in the Divinity of God. With that faith, we harbor Divine sentiments, in our mind and intellect, towards His Names, Forms, Virtues, Pastimes, Abodes, and Saints. If a doubt arises regarding His Divinity, it strikes at the very foundation of our palace of Devotion.

This is exactly what happens to a vast segment of the populace. They engage in devotion to Shree Krishna but then some doubt comes to their minds and their devotion gets crippled. For example, they start thinking that if Shree Krishna was born from Devaki's womb, then He is like the materially bound souls; where is the difference? Or else, they analyze His pastimes with the material intellect and find faults in them.

Hence, the Bhagavad Geeta states, in the verse you have referred to:

जन्म कर्म च मे दिव्यमेवं यो वेत्ति तत्त्वतः।
त्यक्त्वा देहं पुनर्जन्म नैति मामेति सोऽर्जुन।। (गीता ४.९)

*janma karma cha me divyamevaṁ yo vetti tattvataḥ*
*tyaktvā dehaṁ punarjanma naiti māmeti so 'rjuna*

*(Bhagavad Geeta 4.9)*

Shree Krishna says that if your intellect can understand the Divinity of God's birth and activities, then doubts that hinder devotion will not arise, and your love for God will grow quickly. As a result, you will be released from this realm of life and death.

\- *Swamiji*

## The Meaning of "Divine"

**Question:** I have heard the word "Divine" repeatedly mentioned in your *satsaṅgs*. Can you please explain to me what is Divine?

\- *Andrew Singleston, Arlington, Texas*

**Answer:** Dear Andrew, Divine is that which is God-like in nature. God is Divine and anything connected with Him and possessing His nature is also Divine.

However, the absolute import of the word cannot be understood in the materially conditioned state. The materially bound soul has only experienced the realm of Maya since infinite lifetimes. It has no experience till date of anything truly Divine, so how will it understand the word?

The following example will illustrate this point. Let us say, a worm living on the *Neem* tree asks someone, "Madam, can you please explain to me how sweet the *Rasgullā* (Indian sweet made from milk) is?"

The lady replies, "Mr. Worm, have you tasted sugar?"

"No Ma'am!"

"Have you tasted jaggery?"

"No Ma'am!"

"Have you tasted honey?"

"No Ma'am!"

"Have you tasted any sweet thing in your life?"

"No Ma'am! I am a worm of the *Neem* tree. All my life I have only eaten bitter *Neem* leaves."

"Mr. Worm! If you have never tasted anything sweet in your life, how can I explain to you the sweetness of a *Rasgullā*?"

Similarly, the materially bound soul has only experienced the world of Maya all its life. It has never experienced even a speck of the Divine realm of God. So no Saint can truly explain the import of "Divine" to us. Let it suffice to say that it is not material; it is of the nature of God.

- *Swamiji*

## God Never Comes Under Maya

**Question:** Everybody in the material plane is under the influence of Maya. If God takes an Avatar in the world, wouldn't He also come under the influence of Maya?

- *Suryamani Pathak, Baroda, Gujarat*

**Answer:** Dear Suryamani, Understand the answer to your question through the analogy of a jailhouse. There are three kinds of personalities in a prison house:

1. The convicts who are serving their term there. They have been incarcerated against their will.
2. The Warden and employees of the penitentiary. They are not imprisoned, yet out of their own volition, they freely move in and out of the jail.

3. The Governor of the State. In his position as the Executive Head of the State, he has merely come for an administrative inspection of the prison house.

Although all three are in the prison, yet there is a stark contrast in their status. We cannot make a blanket statement that everyone in the prison house is a convict; or that they all are wardens; or that everyone in jail is a Governor. They are all standing in the jailhouse, but in different capacities.

Similarly, this material world is like God's penitentiary. Three kinds of people are present here:

1. The materially bound souls, who have been put in this cycle of life and death because they have turned their backs towards God.
2. The God-realized Saints who are outside the bondage of Maya, but have come into the world just to help the materially bound souls.
3. God Himself, the Proprietor of the jailhouse of Maya, Who occasionally takes an Avatar and descends in the world to accomplish some special work.

As in the previous example, we cannot make a blanket statement that whoever is in the material world is a materially bound soul; or that everyone here is a God-realized Saint; or that all residents of this world are God. They have their own status and personality.

Hence, God does descend on the earth, and that is what we call "Avatar," but it does not mean that He becomes bound by Maya, like us. In fact Maya is the external energy of God and is subservient to Him; it cannot even think of binding Him.

माया परैत्यभिमुखे च विलज्जमाना।। (श्रीमद् भागवतम् २.७.४७)

*māyā paraityabhimukhe cha vilajjamānā*

*(Shreemad Bhagavatam 2.7.47)*

"Maya feels ashamed to even stand before God." Thus, there is no question of God coming under the grips of Maya.

- *Swamiji*

## Reason for God's Pastimes on Earth

**Question:** Many times when we read the *leelas* of God, we are unable to understand the purpose behind them. My question is that why does God do such strange *leelas* on the earth?

*- Keshav Mehta, Mehsana, Gujarat*

**Answer:** Dear Keshav, God's *leelas* are Divine, and hence they are beyond the comprehension of the material intellect. If everything of God could be understood by us, then what would be the difference between Him and us? You cannot hope to know the specific reasons behind His every *leela*, but you can try to comprehend a broad explanation for them.

The primary reason behind God's *leelas* is to provide a basis for the soul to do *Bhakti*. During His Avatar in the world, God manifests His Divine Name, Form, Virtues, Pastimes, Abode, and Associates on the earth plane. These become the basis for the devotion of billions of souls in future. For example, Lord Ram displayed His pastimes ages ago, but even today, innumerable souls remember them, and sing them from the Ramayan, for enhancing their devotion. Hence, the Saint Tulsidas states:

राम एक तापस तिय तारी। नाम कोटि खल कुमति सुधारी।।

*rāma eka tāpasa tiya tārī, nāma koṭi khala kumati sudhārī*

"In His Avatar period, Lord Ram saved only one Ahilya from the stone body. But He left His Divine Name "Ram" behind and billions of fallen souls have saved themselves by taking His Name." By taking an Avatar in the world, the Lord manifested His paraphernalia of Names, Forms, Pastimes, Virtues, and Abode, which the soul can use for fixing the mind upon Him. If God had not descended in the world, the souls would not have had any basis for *Bhakti*, since meditation upon the formless aspect of God is exceedingly difficult.

Hence, the primary reason for the Divine *leelas* of God on the earth is for the welfare of the souls.

## The Bizarre *Leelas* of God

**Question:** I have many questions from the *Purāṇas*. Why did Shree Krishna do the *Mahārās*? Why did Shree Krishna leave the *gopīs* and go to Dwarika? Why did Ram hide and kill Baali? Why does Shiv ji wear a snake around His neck and apply ashes on His body? Why does Vishnu *Bhagavān* sleep on a bed made of a snake?

- *Suresh Udakhe, Nagpur, Maharashtra*

**Answer:** Dear Suresh, That is a lot of questions! Let us systematically find an answer that will resolve all your questions simultaneously, and any similar ones that may arise in future.

There are two kinds of personalities in the world:

1. Those who have not yet attained Bliss, and are hankering for it. All the materially bound souls fall in this category.
2. Those who are relishing perfect Divine Bliss, and have no need to look for it in external objects or personalities. God and the God-realized Saints fall in this category.

Now look at the actions of both these kinds of personalities:

1. Those in the first category are not yet fulfilled; they are searching for Bliss. The motivation behind their every action is self-happiness. Even if they serve others, it is for some hidden self-motive.
2. Those in the second category are already absorbed in Divine Bliss. They have nothing to attain, and nowhere to reach. So, either they will do nothing, or if they ever do anything, it will be for the welfare of others, not for themselves.

Hence, the simple answer to all your questions, regarding why any Avatar of God did anything, is that it was for the welfare of the souls. Now, it is a different matter that we may not be able to comprehend what was the welfare through a particular action. But that should not be surprising to us! After all, how large is God's intellect, and in comparison, how small is ours?

Suppose that a primary school student were to go to Albert Einstein, and ask him how he arrived at his equation $E=mc^2$. Einstein could question him, "Do you know polar integration?"

"No Sir!"

"Do you know Calculus?"

"Sir, I have never heard of it!"

"Do you at least know Algebra?"

"No! All I know is how to count two plus two on my fingers."

Einstein would probably say, "In that case I cannot explain my Relativity Equation to you."

"Really, you cannot explain it to me? That means your theory is wrong." If the boy were to reach such a conclusion, how presumptuous and inaccurate that would be!

Similarly, the *Mahārās* of Shree Krishna is in the tenth canto of the Shreemad Bhagavatam. If we want to jump straight there without having even realized that we are *ātmā*, not the body, it will be equally presumptuous. We must begin understanding spirituality from Grade One. First, from the Bhagavad Geeta, we should appreciate that we are the soul and not the body. With this knowledge, we must learn to detach ourselves from the world.

Then, we should start relishing Divine Love from the Bhagavatam, which begins where the Bhagavad Geeta ends. The *Mahārās* is in the tenth canto of the Bhagavatam, and so it is a post-doctoral topic. By gradually progressing in our devotion, we will reach the point where we will develop an understanding of the *Mahārās* of Shree Krishna.

People ask me about Lord Ram hiding and killing Baali. I ask a counter question, "How do you know Ram killed Baali in that fashion?"

They reply, "It is written in the Ramayan."

I ask them again, "If you believe what is mentioned in the Ramayan to be true, then you must also believe that Ram is God, since that is also written there."

They reply, "We do not accept that Ram is God, because we do not believe what is written in the Ramayan."

"Then you should also not believe that Ram hid and killed Baali. So your question itself is incorrect."

Others reply, "Of course we believe Ram to be God, because it is written in the Ramayan."

"If you do accept Ram as God, there can be no doubt about His actions, for God cannot make any mistakes."

The best way to derive benefit from the pastimes described in the *Purāṇas* and other scriptures is to not use the intellect in analyzing them. Simply relish them with the mind. Use the intellect to understand that there is no happiness in the world, so that you can detach the mind from here.

*- Swamiji*

## Faith in the Divine Pastimes of God

**Question:** First of all, I am at a loss to find suitable words to express my heartfelt thanks for receiving your greeting card on the auspicious day of Divali. The card showed Lord Krishna celebrating along with His friends both *Gopas* and *Gopīs* by floating lighted *diyās* in the pond. My question is how to spiritually interpret the *gopas* and *gopīs*, the *diyās*, and the festival of Divali?

*- Rajesh Kumar Tiwari, Yamuna Vihar, Delhi*

**Answer:** Dear Rajesh, Often intellectuals have a tendency to not accept the *Leelas* of God as Divine, and instead make figurative interpretations of them. For example, they say that the Ramayan did not actually take place. Seeta is just a symbol of devotion. Hanuman is a symbol of faith. Ayodhya is within your body itself, etc. In this way, they draw figurative interpretations of all the pastimes.

However, this defeats the purpose of the pastimes because it destroys the Divine sentiments towards them. If we do so then we will not be able to take advantage of these *leelas* to fix our mind on God and increase our love.

Hence, if you wish to relish the Bliss of Divine love then stop interpreting them and simply rejoice in them, as the amazing *leelas* of the Supreme Lord.

- *Swamiji*

## Taking the Name of God

**Question:** We give respect to elders in the world. So we do not call them by their names. But, we call God by His Names like Radha, Krishna, etc. Isn't calling God's Name similar to insulting Him?

- *Manoj Trehan, Houston, Texas*

**Answer:** Dear Manoj, Taking God's Name is a simple way to remember Him. It is an easy method of engaging in devotion. One can take the Name along with performing one's worldly duties. Chaitanya Mahaprabhu said:

खाइते शुइते यथा तथा नाम लय।
काल देश नियम नाहि, सर्व सिद्धि हय।। (चैतन्य चरितामृत)

*khāite śhuite yathā tathā nāma laya*
*kāla deśha niyama nāhi, sarva siddhi haya*
*(Chaitanya Charitāmṛita Antya 20.18)*

"Taking the Name of God is so easy because there are no rules for it; one can do it even while eating, walking, resting, etc., and in this way attain Divine Love."

In the Jewish tradition, they do not take God's Name for exactly the reason you have given. They feel it would be insulting to Him. However, the Vedic understanding is that when we take God's Name, He feels delighted that we are increasing our love for Him.

Chanting the Name is also a way of expressing our love for Him. Many devotees chant the Names in groups, which is called *saṅkīrtan*. Jagadguru Shree Kripaluji Maharaj says:

राधे राधे बोल नित, करु राधे को ध्यान।
ऐहैँ निज गोलोक तजि, भाजत श्याम सुजान।। (भक्ति शतक)

*rādhe rādhe bola nita, karu rādhe ko dhyāna*
*aihaiñ nija goloka taji, bhājata śhyāma sujāna (Bhakti Śhatak)*

"Always chant the name of "Radha" and meditate upon Her Divine Form. Shree Krishna will be so pleased that He will leave Golok and come running to you."

- *Swamiji*

14

# Science of Devotion

## *Bhakti* will Cleanse the Mind

**Question:** In today's materialistic world, the soul takes a beating, and the extent depends on the society, the profession, the community and each person's ability to bear it. How does one cleanse or heal his soul?

- *Ajay Sharma, San Bruno, California*

**Answer:** Dear Ajay, You are the soul, which is a part of God, and hence by nature you are perpetually Divine. You do not need to cleanse the soul. The problem is that the soul is identifying with the body, mind, and intellect. Hence, when the mind feels tormented, the soul experiences the misery. For example, if someone cuts your head in your dream, even though the dream is not a reality, you will experience the suffering until you wake up from the dream. Similarly, the Divine soul experiences the distress of the mind in the materially conditioned state because it identifies with it.

So when you say that the soul takes a beating, what you mean is that the mind takes a beating, and the soul experiences the pain vicariously. Once the mind is sufficiently cleansed, the soul will be able to perceive the distinction between itself and the mind, and distance itself from its dualities. Hence, we must endeavor to cleanse the mind.

Many materialists too are awake to this need for purifying the mind, since the soul naturally feels disconcerted by an impure mind and yearns to experience the state of purity that is natural to it. A plethora of techniques and self-help books are available in the world for practicing positive thinking in its various forms and connotations. However, all these techniques have very limited effectiveness, and the results achieved are temporary. We must remember that the mind is made from Maya, which is God's energy, and it cannot be conquered by self-effort alone. The mind can be permanently and totally healed only by the Grace of God.

So the most powerful practice for cleansing the mind is to engage it in *Bhakti*, or love of God. That is the verdict of all the Vedic literatures and the essence of all religions. Shree Krishna explains in the Bhagavad Geeta that Maya has three *guṇas—sattva*, *rajas*, and *tamas*. These three *guṇas*, or modes, are also present in the mind, which fluctuates between these three *guṇas*. Based on the *guṇa* of the environment or the object to which one is attached, the corresponding *guṇa* becomes dominant in the mind. However, God is beyond these three *guṇas*. He is Divine, and so when we attach our mind to Him, it too rises beyond the three *guṇas* and becomes Divine.

The Ramayan states:

प्रेम भगति जल बिनु रघुराई। अभिअंतर मल कबहुँ न जाई।।

*prema bhagati jala binu raghurāī, abhiantara mala kahabhuñ na jāī (Ramayan)*

"Until we wash our mind in the water of love of God, its dirt will never go."

The Bhagavatam states:

धर्मः सत्यदयोपेतो विद्या वा तपसान्विता।
मद्भक्त्यापेतमात्मानं न सम्यक् प्रपुनाति हि।। (भागवतम्)

*dharmaḥ satyadayopeto vidyā vā tapasānvitā*
*madbhaktyāpetamātmānaṁ na samyak prapunāti hi*
*(Shreemad Bhagavatam 11.14.22)*

"We may follow all the rules of proper conduct, we may perform severe austerities, and we may accumulate the most esoteric knowledge, but without *Bhakti*, none of these practices will suffice in cleansing the mind."

So, do try to understand and sincerely practice the various facets of the science of devotion to God. Use that knowledge to attach your mind to Him, relishing the Bliss of Divine Love, and very soon you will experience the mind being elevated and cleansed from endless lifetimes of impurities.

- *Swamiji*

## The Ultimate Goal of Humans

**Question:** Is *Bhagavad Prāpti* and liberation from the cycle of life and death alone the aim of life?

- *Narendra Mehta, Mehsana, Gujarat*

**Answer:** Dear Narendra, The goal of *sādhanā* is higher than liberation, and in fact, even higher than God-realization. The goal of life is to attain Divine Love for God, with which we may engage in His Eternal Loving service.

The Sage Ved Vyas writes:

धर्मः प्रोज्झित कैतवोऽत्र परमो निर्मत्सराणां सतां। (भागवतम्)

*dharmaḥ projjhita kaitavo 'tra paramo nirmatsarāṇāṁ satāṁ*

*(Shreemad Bhagavatam 1.1.2)*

He says in the second verse of the Shreemad Bhagavatam that in this scripture he will go beyond *Dharm*, *Arth*, *Kām*, *Mokṣh*, and explain the ultimate goal of life, which is the attainment of Divine Love for God. Chaitanya Mahaprabhu called Divine Love as "*Purushārth Śhiromaṇi*" or the highest attainable objective.

The intriguing thing is that when you make Divine Love as your goal, all other things will automatically be added to you:

राम भजत सोइ मुकुति गोसाईं। अनइच्छित आवइ बरिआईं।।

*rāma bhajata soi mukuti gosāī, anaichchhita āvai bariāīñ*

*(Ramayan)*

"If you get Divine Love of God, liberation will ensue automatically." Appreciating this secret, decide upon making *Bhakti* as your goal.

*- Swamiji*

## Difference between Divine Love and Worldly Love

**Question:** What is Divine Love and how is it different from worldly love?

*- Beverley Whitworth, Houston, Texas*

**Answer:** Dear Beverley, Divine Love is that where the desire is simply to give...give...and give. There is no selfish desire for anything in return. Worldly love is that where the desire is to take... take...and take. It is a selfish affection for one's own happiness.

Chaitanya Mahaprabhu compared the two to sunlight and darkness:

कामेर तात्पर्य निज सम्भोग केवल।
कृष्ण सुख तात्पर्य मात्र प्रेम तो प्रबल।।
लोक धर्म, वेद धर्म, देह धर्म, कर्म।
लज्जा, धैर्य, देह सुख, आत्म सुख मर्म।।
सर्व त्याग करये करे कृष्णेर भजन।
कृष्ण सुख हेतु करे प्रेमेर सेवन।।
अतएव काम प्रेमे बहुत अन्तर।
काम अन्धतम, प्रेम निर्मल भास्कर।।
(चैतन्य चरितामृत आदि ४.१६६, १६७, १६९ एवम् १७१)

*kāmera tātparya nija sambhoga kevala*
*kṛiṣhṇa sukha tātparya mātra prema to prabala*
*loka dharma, veda dharma, deha dharma, karma*
*lajjā, dhairya, deha sukha, ātma sukha marma*
*sarva tyāga karaye kare kṛiṣhṇera bhajana*
*kṛiṣhṇa sukha hetu kare premera sevana*
*ataeva kāma preme bahuta antara*
*kāma andhatama, prema nirmala bhāskara*
*(Chaitanya Charitāmṛita Ādi.4.166, 167, 169, And 171)*

"Worldly love (lust) is for the sake of self-pleasure while Divine Love is for the sake of Shree Krishna's pleasure. Reject all kinds of religiosity to practice devotion to Shree Krishna. Relish this Divine

Love for the sake of His happiness. There is a great difference between Divine Love and lust; the former is like the rays of sunlight, while the latter is like darkness."

*- Swamiji*

## Asking God for His Love is not Selfishness

**Question:** According to the philosophy of Shree Maharajji, one should love God unconditionally. But on the other hand, he also directs us to beg Him for His Grace. This is why I am confused because in unconditional love we should not ask God for anything. Would you please reply to me, sparing a few moments of your precious time?

*- Hemant Maske, Mumbai, Maharashtra*

**Answer:** Dear Hemant, Shree Maharajji teaches us to engage in devotion for the pleasure of Radha Krishna and to make Their service as our goal. However, we can only serve God if we possess love for Him. God is not interested in our mechanical actions; He is pleased by the love of our heart. The more devotion we have, the more our service will be satisfying Him.

So with the goal of serving God and making Him happy, we can ask for Grace, Divine knowledge, Divine Love, renunciation from the world, etc. Since our objective is the satisfaction of God and Guru, our asking will not be considered selfish.

The entire philosophy of Divine Love as explained by Shree Maharajji, can be summarized in the following few aphorisms:

- Our goal is the selfless Divine service of Shree Radha Krishna.
- That selfless Divine service can only be performed when we possess Divine Love.
- Divine Love will be bestowed upon us by God and Guru when we cleanse our heart.
- To cleanse our heart, we will have to do *sādhanā* under the guidance of the Guru.
- While putting in our best efforts in doing *sādhanā*, we must

pray to God and Guru to bestow Their Grace for success in it.

*- Swamiji*

## God Knows What is Best for Us

**Question:** When we ask something of God (be it *Mokṣh* or Vaikunth or Golok or Saket Lok), aren't we telling God that we know better than Him what is good for us?

*- Neeraj Rai, Ranchi, Bihar*

**Answer:** Dear Neeraj, Your question is very apt. We do not need to ask God for anything. It is best to leave it on Him to decide what He wishes to give us. If we ask with our intellect, it is highly likely that we will ask for something inferior. For example, bring a little child to a jewelry shop, and put a chocolate in front of him. Then ask him, "My son, take whatever you want." What do you think the child will pick up? Obviously, his hand will go for the chocolates, since he has no idea of the value of gold and diamonds.

Similarly, we too are like little children in the realm of spirituality, and we have no idea of what all is available in the dominion of God. So if we ask from Him, it will be only to the extent that our tiny intellects can understand. Since endless lifetimes, we have pursued worldly happiness, and it is likely that we will ask God for that alone. Instead if we leave it upon Him, He will decide what is best for us and then give it even without our asking for it.

There is a Hindi saying in this regard:

मेरी चाही मत करो मैं मूरख अज्ञान,
तेरी चाही में प्रभु है मेरा कल्याण।

*merī chāhī mata karo main mūrakha agyāna,*
*terī chāhī meñ prabhu hai merā kalyāṇ*

"O my Master! Please do not deal with me according to my desires. It is in the fulfillment of Your desires that I will be benefitted."

However, asking from God is not necessarily with the mouth alone. He notes the inner desires of our mind. So it is important to become selfless from within our mind, and not merely by our words.

The Guru and scriptures teach us to ask for certain things, as a part of the training of the mind. For example, by asking: प्रेम भिक्षां देही। *prema bhikshāṁ dehī* (Give me Divine Love), we train the mind to hanker for Divine Love. By asking God for His service, we train the mind to yearn for the opportunity to serve Him. By asking for His Grace, we train the mind to become humble and depend upon His Grace rather than self-effort. To ask for the proper things in accordance with the instructions of the scriptures is not wrong; it is a way of increasing our love and service attitude towards God and Guru.

In this way, asking for the proper things becomes a part of the practice of training the mind in devotion. Simultaneously, internally we should maintain this attitude, "My Lord! I do not know what is good for me. You please decide and do as You wish."

*- Swamiji*

## Five Sentiments of Devotion

**Question:** How can the *gopīs'* love for Krishna be interpreted in the path of devotion?

*- Seema Behera, Bhubaneshwar, Odisha*

**Answer:** Dear Seema, In the chapter "Secret of God's Descension", I have explained that we should not make figurative interpretations of the Divine pastimes of God, rather we should take them as literal and true. Accordingly, let me explain the significance in devotion of the love of the *gopīs*.

The word for devotion in Sanskrit is "*Upāsanā*", which means to go and sit close to God. Now, the Lord is all-pervading and also seated in our hearts; how will we go close to Him? Here, closeness implies proximity of the mind with God. There are five *bhāvs* (sentiments) of devotion that help us develop proximity with Him:

1. *Śhānt bhāv* or the sentiment of Majesty: "Shree Krishna is my King."
2. *Dāsya bhāv* or the sentiment of Servitude: "Shree Krishna is my Master."

3. *Sakhya bhāv* or the Fraternal sentiment: "Shree Krishna is my Friend."
4. *Vātsalya bhāv* or the Parental sentiment: "I am Shree Krishna's mother or father."
5. *Mādhurya bhāv* or the Conjugal sentiment: "Shree Krishna is my Beloved."

These sentiments get us sequentially closer to God. The *gopīs* loved Shree Krishna as their Beloved, and hence they felt intimately close to Him. This is considered the highest sentiment of devotion. It is distinguished from the sentiment of worldly lovers by the trait of selflessness. The nature of *gopī prem* is described as follows:

स्वसुख वासना गन्ध लेश शून्य श्री कृष्ण सुखैक तात्पर्यमयी सेवा।

*svasukha vāsanā gandha leśha śhūnya*
*śhrī kṛiṣhṇa sukhaika tātparyamayī sevā*

"The devotion of the *gopīs* is such that even the slightest aroma of the trace of the desire for self-happiness does not exist. The only goal is the pleasure of Shree Krishna." Hence the love of the *gopīs* has been eulogized by many great personalities. The Creator Brahma states:

षष्ठि वर्ष सहस्त्राणि मया तप्तं तपः पुरा।
नन्दगोपव्रजस्त्रीणां पादरेणुपलब्धये।
तथापि न मया प्राप्तास्तासां वै पादरेणवः।। (बृहद् वामनपुराण)

*ṣhaṣhṭhi varṣha sahasrāṇi mayā taptaṁ tapaḥ purā*
*nandagopavrajastrīṇāṁ pāda-reṇupalabdhaye*
*tathāpi na mayā prāptāstāsāṁ vai pādareṇavaḥ*
*(Bṛihad Vāmana Purāṇa)*

"I practiced austerities for sixty-thousand years to attain the dust of the lotus feet of the *gopīs*, but I could not succeed."

The great *Gyānī* Uddhav said:

आसामहो चरणरेणुजुषामहंस्यां वृन्दावने किमपिगुल्मलतौषधीनाम्।
या दुस्त्यजं स्वजनमार्यपथं च हित्वा भेजुर्मुकुन्दपदवीं श्रुतिभिर्विमृग्याम्।।
(भागवतम् १०.४७.६१)

*āsāmaho charaṇareṇujuṣhāmahansyāṁ*

*vṛindāvane kimapigulmalatauṣhadhīnām*
*yā dustyajaṁ svajanamāryapathaṁ cha hitvā*
*bhejurmukundapadavīṁ śhrutibhirvimṛigyām*
*(Shreemad Bhagavatam 10.47.61)*

"O Shree Krishna! In my next life, do not give me a human birth; make me a blade of grass in Your land of Braj, so that I may attain the dust of the lotus feet of the *gopīs* and become eligible to receive Your Divine Love, just as they possess."

The great Āchārya of *Bhakti*, Narad Muni states:

यथा ब्रज गोपिकानाम्। (नारद भक्ति सूत्र २१)

*yathā braja gopikānām (Nārada Bhakti Sūtra 21)*

"The highest ideal of devotion was manifest in the *gopīs*."

Chaitanya Mahaprabhu was a staunch *sanyāsī* (renunciant), and strictly followed the rules of the *sanyās āśhram* (renounced order of life). Yet he held the devotion of the *gopīs*, the damsels of Braj, to be the highest sentiment of devotion, and he relished savoring and hearing about the nectar of gopī *bhāv*."

Jagadguru Nimbarkacharya too was a great and scholarly *sanyāsī*. He also held the love of the *gopīs* to be the highest state of devotion. Mahaprabhu Vallabhacharya practiced devotion in *Vātsalya bhāv* (parental sentiment), but in the later part of his life, he moved to *mādhurya bhāv*, the sentiment of the *gopīs*.

Hence, we see how the scriptures and the great Saints have alike praised the devotion of the *gopīs*. We should not misinterpret it to be some kind of material love.

- *Swamiji*

## Divine Love is a Gift of God

**Question:** Is *Bhakti* something that is bestowed upon the soul by God's Grace, or is it something that is developed in the heart by *puruśhārth* (self-effort)?

- *Gunjan Pandey, Middletown, Connecticut*

**Answer:** Dear Gunjan, Divine Love is a special power of God. It is not created by *Sādhanā*. It is received by the soul through the Grace of God.

The highest power of God is *Yogmāyā* (Divine Internal Energy). That *Yogmāyā* has three attributes: *Sat*, *Chit*, and *Ānand*. The highest of these is *Ānand Brahm* (the Bliss aspect of God). The essence of *Ānand* is *Hlādinī Śhakti* (the power that gives Bliss to God). The essence of *Hlādinī Śhakti* is *Premā Śhakti* (the power of Divine Love).

You do not need to remember the names; let it suffice to bear in mind that *Premā Śhakti* (Divine Love) is the essence of the essence of the essence of the highest power of God. It is such a power that God Himself becomes a servant of whoever possesses it.

अहं भक्तपराधीनो ह्यस्वतन्त्र इव द्विज।
साधुभिर्ग्रस्तहृदयो भक्तैर्भक्तजनप्रियः।। (भागवतम् ९.४.६३)

*ahaṁ bhaktaparādhīno hyasvatantra iva dvija*
*sādhubhirgrastahṛidayo bhaktairbhaktajanapriyaḥ*
*(Shreemad Bhagavatam 9.4.63)*

Shree Krishna says: "I am not independent; I have been enslaved by My devotees. My *Bhaktas* have purchased My heart and are very dear to Me."

Such a power, which is the highest power of God, cannot be attained by *puruśhārth* (self-effort). It is only received by the Grace of the God-realized Saints who already possess it. Lord Ram told Lakshman:

भगति तात अनुपम सुखमूला। मिलइ जो सन्त होइँ अनुकूला।।

*bhagati tāta anupama sukhamūlā, milai jo santa hoiñ anukūlā*
*(Ramayan)*

"*Bhakti* is the source of incomparable Divine Bliss. It is obtained when the Guru bestows His Grace upon the soul."

However, we do need to keep in mind that the Grace of God and the Guru is not a whimsical or irrational occurrence. It is bestowed when we prepare the vessel of the heart for receiving it. The heart is cleansed by doing *Sādhan Bhakti* (Preparatory Devotion).

Thus, we need to do *Sādhan Bhakti* and then by the Grace of the Guru, we will get *Siddha Bhakti* (Divine Love).

- *Swamiji*

## *Siddhis* and Manifestations of *Prem*

**Question:** I was reading this book where different manifestations of *Prem* (Divine Love) are mentioned, like crying, smelling good aromas, hearings sounds....are they not same as *siddhis* (mystical powers) obtained through *Haṭha yoga/Rāja yoga*? It is mentioned in the book that one gets immersed in those and can feel the presence of God. But *siddhis* are some things that are gained in the process and not to be entangled in for they lead to materialism again! How does one distinguish?

*- Seema Behera, Bhubaneshwar, Odisha*

**Answer:** Dear Seema, The symptoms of Divine Love are entirely different from the *siddhis* (mystic powers) that are attained through *Haṭha Yog*.

When the love in the heart swells exceedingly, occasionally it manifests in any or all eight symptoms, called *aṣhṭa sāttvic bhāv* (eight signs of devotion). This happens either in immense longing for God, or in the unlimited Bliss of union with Him. Understand this through the example of a pressure cooker. When the pressure increases within it, the pressure cooker whistle is pushed up and the steam shoots out. Similarly, when the loving sentiments in the heart of the devotee become uncontrollable, they manifest externally in the following eight sentiments:

1. *Stambh*: The body, mind, and intellect become stupefied in love.
2. *Sved*: The body sweats due to the temperature of the love within.
3. *Romañch*: The hair of the body stand on end due to thrilling.
4. *Svar Bhed*: The voice becomes choked with loving sentiments.
5. *Vepathu*: The body starts trembling in ecstasy.
6. *Vaivarṇya*: The color of the face fades due to the intensity of the sentiments.

7. *Aśhru*: Tears begin rolling out of the eyes profusely.
8. *Pralay*: The mind and intellect stop working and the devotee faints in Divine trance.

These are the external symptoms of the love in the heart of the devotee. They are not to be confused with the *siddhis* that are attained by the *Haṭha Yog sādhanā*.

In *Haṭha Yog*, when the mind gets concentrated, mystical abilities start developing:

अणिमा महिमा मूर्तेर्लघिमा प्राप्तिरिन्द्रियैः।
प्राकाम्यं श्रुतदृष्टेषु शक्तिप्रेरणमीशिता।। (भागवतम् ११.१५.४)

*aṇimā mahimā mūrterlaghimā prāptirindriyaiḥ*
*prākāmyaṁ śhrutadṛiṣhṭeṣhu śhaktipreraṇamīśhitā*
*(Shreemad Bhagavatam 11.15.4)*

There are eight mystic abilities mentioned in the scriptures, such as making one's body small, enlarging one's body, manifesting some object from elsewhere, reading someone's mind, becoming light as a feather, etc. These mystic abilities appear to be very fascinating and attractive to the neophyte aspirant. However, they can divert one from the main goal of God-realization. They can also lead to pride and attachment in the world. Hence, the *sādhak* is warned to stay away from them; and even if they develop, not to indulge in them.

Hence, the Sage Ved Vyas states:

न योग सिद्धीरपुनर्भवं वा मय्यर्पितात्मेच्छति मद् विनान्यत्।।

*na yoga siddhirpunarbhavaṁ vā*
*mayyarpitātmechchhati mad vinānyat*
*(Shreemad Bhagavatam 11.14.14)*

"O Lord! Those who have taken the shelter of Your lotus feet do not desire the *siddhis* of *Haṭha Yog*, and do not even hanker for liberation."

*- Swamiji*

# 15

# The Guru

## The Need of a Guru on the Spiritual Path

**Question:** God is seated in our hearts. What is the need of a Guru to meet Him?

- *Subrat Roy, Monroeville, Philadelphia*

**Answer:** Dear Subrat, The Vedas are the word of God, in which God has Himself taught the necessity of a Guru:

तद्विज्ञानार्थं स गुरुमेवाभिगच्छेत् समित्पाणि: श्रोत्रियं ब्रह्मनिष्ठम्।।

*tadvigyānārthaṁ sa gurumevābhigachchhet samitpāṇiḥ*
*śhrotriyaṁ brahmaniṣhṭham (Muṇḍakopaniṣhad 1.2.12)*

"To know God, approach a Spiritual Master, who is both—well-versed in the knowledge of the scriptures and also seated on the platform of God-realization. Serve him with faith and humility."

We are separated from God, not because of physical distance but because of the ignorance within us, which exists since infinite lifetimes. Because of ignorance, although we are the soul, we are thinking of ourselves to be the body; although we are immortal, we are mortified of death; although we will leave everything behind in the world one day, we are thinking of our possessions to be permanent. We do perceive the existence of defects such as anger, greed, lust, envy, and hatred; and we wish to get rid of them, but are unable to. This is proof of the existence of nescience within us. The Sage Ved Vyas writes:

अज्ञानमेवास्य ही मूल कारणम्।

*agyānamevāsya hī mūla kāraṇam*

"The cause of all our miseries is ignorance."

Thus, to overcome miseries and to reach God, we need knowledge. That knowledge cannot be attained simply by the thinking power of our intellect. The reason for this is simple. The intellect itself is where the ignorance resides, and so its own thinking capacity is inherently incapable of destroying its ignorance.

What other source of spiritual knowledge do we have? There is an immense treasure-house of knowledge in the Vedic scriptures, but these are again impossible to understand merely by the analysis of our intellect. Just as God is Divine, the scriptures too are Divine. If on our own, we attempt to comprehend them, we end up confused, for there are many apparent contradictions in them. Hence, the scriptures themselves instruct us that they must be studied under the guidance of a true Guru.

तस्माद् गुरुं प्रपद्यते जिज्ञासुः श्रेय उत्तमम्। (श्रीमद् भागवतम्)

*tasmād guruṁ prapadyate jigyāsuḥ śhreya uttamam*

*(Shreemad Bhagavatam 11.3.21)*

"One who is desirous of knowing the Truth must surrender to a Guru." The Guru should be someone who is well-versed in the knowledge of the scriptures and situated on the platform of God-realization."

- *Swamiji*

## Who is a True Guru?

**Question:** In the Indian culture, we all have heard hundreds of times since childhood that we need a Guru. But is there any definition of who a true Guru is? Also, please explain the difference between Guru and *Sadguru*.

- *Gurucharan Baweja, Vancouver, Canada*

**Answer:** Dear Gurucharan, The word "guru" has now been adopted by the English language as well, and so we hear terms such as Marketing guru, Economics guru, Finance guru, etc. However, when you refer to the true Guru, you are enquiring about the spiritual connotation of the word as described in the scriptures. The meaning of the word "Guru" is:

गु शब्दस्त्वन्धकारस्यात् रु शब्दस्तन्निरोधकः।
अन्धकार निरोधत्वात् गुरुरित्यभिधीयते।। (अद्वय तारकोपनिषद् १६)

*gu śhabdastvandhakārasyāt ru śhabdastannirodhakaḥ*
*andhakāra nirodhatvāt gururityabhidhīyate*
*(Advaya Tārakopanishad 16)*

"The syllable "*gu*" means "darkness," and "*ru*" means "to destroy." Hence, one who dispels our nescience and brings to us the light of true wisdom is the Guru.

The true Guru must have two qualifications. Firstly, he or she should possess theoretical knowledge of the scriptures—this is called *Śhrotriya*. Secondly, he or she should have realized that knowledge and be seated in the Truth—this is called *Brahm Niṣhṭh*. Hence, a true Guru is one who is both—*Śhrotriya* and *Brahm Niṣhṭh*.

In these, the second criterion is most important, i.e. the Guru must be God-realized. Only one who has attained God can help others attain Him. If one is a beggar himself, how can he give money to others; if one has no knowledge himself, how can he teach others? If one has not attained the Bliss of Divine love, how can he give it to others?

Hence, a Guru who has attained God is the true Guru, and such a Spiritual Master is called "*Sadguru*," or "One who is seated in the Truth."

\- *Swamiji*

## The Process of Finding a True Guru

**Question:** My friends and acquaintances all try and pull me to their *sampradāyas* (religious sects). They all praise their own Gurus.

It causes confusion in my mind, and I do not know how to choose my Guru. Please tell me the process for finding my Guru.

*- Nandkishore Goyal, Austin, Texas*

**Answer:** Dear Nandkishore, There is a saying in Hindi:

पानी पियो छान के, गुरु बनाओ जानके।

*pānī piyo chhānake, guru banāo jānake*

"Drink water only after filtering it; make a Guru only after carefully knowing him." We must not accept anyone as our Guru, merely because of a friend's suggestion; we must ourselves recognize someone as a true Guru, and only then should we surrender to him.

However, just as it is not possible for a First Grade student to evaluate the capability of a college teacher, similarly, it is not easy to recognize a Guru, who is a Divine personality, while we are only beginning the path of spirituality. Yet, there are certain characteristics that provide helpful indications:

1. The true Guru's words are very impacting. Although we may have heard and read the same knowledge many times without being moved by it, when we hear the same words from the mouth of a God-realized Saint, they change us from within. We can perceive that there is something different in the way the Guru expounds the knowledge, which makes it so impacting. The reason for this is that the *Sadguru* does not merely elucidate what he has read in books; he explains from the depths of personal realization. Hence, it goes deep into the hearts of the listeners.

2. Whatever doubts we have on the spiritual path, if we place them before the Guru, he or she can easily resolve them and dispel our confusions. A mere theoretical scholar of the scriptures cannot do this. Scholarly learning without practical *sādhanā* only increases the confusions, since there are many scriptures and each states different spiritual principles. The theoretical scholar becomes confused with the apparent contradictions. However, the *Sadguru* possesses realized knowledge, for he or she has seen the Truth, and is able to reveal it with the benefit of experience.

3. A true Guru does not give his disciple material allurements. Rather, he teaches that worldly attainments are not the goal. Nowadays, many so-called saints claim to have a magic formula for removing all the material miseries and bestowing money, wealth, prestige, etc. on their followers. Allured by such false statements, people flock to them in thousands. We must beware of such imposters who have not yet even understood that detachment from the world, and not material attainments, is the goal of spiritual life.
4. If we associate with a true Guru, we will naturally find ourselves getting attached to God and detached from the world. Just as when we feel cold and walk towards fire, as we go closer to the fire, we naturally experience the cold going away and heat entering the body. Similarly, the God-realized Saint is like a fireball of God-consciousness. If we associate with him, we will experience the Divine consciousness rubbing on us as well.
5. The above points are all helpful in recognizing a Saint, but the strongest indication will come from God Himself. When He sees in us a sincere desire to meet Him, He will guide us to a true Guru. And when the inspiration comes from God, we will know it by its intensity; our heart will urge us that we have found the Guru we were looking for. This point will be further discussed in the answer to the next question.

*- Swamiji*

## God Helps Us Find the Guru

**Question:** There is an age-old saying: "When you are ready the teacher will appear." Swamiji, what is that "readiness" required for the GURU to appear? With prayers.....

*- Seema Behera, Bhubaneshwar, Odisha*

**Answer:** Dear Seema, The Vedic scriptures repeatedly teach the need to surrender to a Guru, for attaining God. However, the question that stumps a seeker is how to find a true Guru. Where should we go?

Fortunately, God helps the sincere seeker in this task. He is seated in everyone's heart, and so when He sees that we are ready, He not only brings us in contact with a genuine Guru, but also creates our faith towards the Guru by inspiring us with the feeling, "Yes! This is the personality whom I was searching for." Without this inspiration that comes so strongly from within, we may stand before the Guru, and yet not recognize him as a true Saint. Or we may recognize his Divinity, but feel no motivation to surrender to him. But when God bestows His Grace, He inspires us and creates strong faith in the Guru. Hence, it is said that when God sees we are ready, we find our Spiritual Master.

However, you have asked what that "readiness" is. Here, readiness means a sincere aspiration to attain God. We must firmly decide that our goal is God-realization, and we must desire it intensely. When God sees this readiness in any soul, He creates our connection with the Guru.

Often people search for spiritual teachers, but their desire for God is mixed with material aspirations. In accordance with their motive, their faith is created in unauthentic spiritual teachers who pander to their material desires. After many years, such seekers realize that their guru was not perfect, and they feel they have been cheated. But it was their own insincere aspiration that was to blame for their developing faith in a wrong personality.

Hence, the best way to find a genuine Spiritual Master is to develop an intense yearning for God. When He sees this "readiness" in our heart, He will arrange for us to meet our teacher.

- *Swamiji*

## Regarding Changing of Gurus

**Question:** I was very inspired by my Guruji when I first came to the path seven years ago. I began practicing Yoga and Meditation as he taught me. But I did not make any progress. I read the *śhāstras* and realized that his path was not for me. I am attracted to *Bhakti*, but I am scared that I have already made a Guru, and I will be committing a sin if I change Gurus. Please resolve my dilemma.

- *Tanushree Shukla, Gwalior, Madhya Pradesh*

**Answer:** Dear Tanushree, You have made innumerable gurus in endless past lifetimes. So you have already been changing gurus in every life.

The human form is given to us for attaining knowledge, and to do so, you have the right to keep looking for a true Guru. In the process, it may sometimes happen that you begin the journey with some spiritual teacher, but then realize that he is not a *Sadguru*, or that your *sanskārs* do not suit the path that he teaches. In such a case, you have the right to move on and look elsewhere.

When you are sick and go to a doctor, if the doctor's treatment does not work, you see another doctor, or even try alternative systems such as Yogic Therapy, Homoeopathy, Naturopathy, or Ayurveda. You do not say, "Well, I have gotten a doctor now, and whether I live or die from his treatment, I can't change him." Then why should you think, "I have surrendered to a guru, and now, and whether I go to heaven or hell, I can't change him."

However, once you have found a God-realized Saint, and you are convinced about his attainments, then you should stop moving from Saint to Saint. Instead, you should now surrender yourself to the genuine Spiritual Master and do *sādhanā* under his guidance.

*- Swamiji*

## The Guru *Mantra*

**Question:** What is the special power in the Guru *mantra* that is given in the ear of the disciple at the time of *dīkṣhā* (initiation)? Is it compulsory to receive a *mantra* for our devotion? Why are we told to keep it a secret and what will happen if we tell our Guru *mantra* to friends?

*- Nithya Bodhananda, Bangalore, Karnataka*

**Answer:** Dear Nithya Bodhananda, True *dīkṣhā* is not merely the giving of a *mantra* in the ear of the disciple. True *dīkṣhā* means to give the Divine power of God to the disciple. It should result in liberation from Maya, attainment of Divine Knowledge, Love, and Bliss, and initiation into the eternal pastimes of God. Such *dīkṣhā* is given by the Guru only when the disciple has fully cleansed his or her mind through the practice of *Sādhan Bhakti*, or preparatory devotion.

Understand this point through an example. Let us say, you are making a house. You complete all the electrical fitting—the wiring, the fans, lights, switches, meter boxes, etc. But there is still no electricity in your house. That is because you do not have the connection from the power house. The mechanic from the Electric Company then comes and joins the main wire of your house to the external power line, and instantly, there is light in your house. Just as you first prepared your house, and then got the connection, similarly you will first have to do *sādhanā* under the guidance of the Guru to purify your heart and then you will receive *dīkṣhā*, or the Divine power from the Guru.

The problem arises when people do not want to purify their hearts. They look for shortcuts whereby they can retain all their worldly desires, and yet attain God. Therefore, claims of magic *mantras*, tantras, and yantras are very appealing to them. And Gurus who offer such allurements become very popular. But we must remember that until the heart is totally cleansed, we will not receive the Divine Grace which is necessary for God-realization. And to cleanse the heart, we can chant any name of God; there is no need of a special *mantra*.

What are these Guru *mantras* all about? They are Sanskrit words that usually mean things like: "O Shree Krishna, I surrender to You," "O Shree Ram, I offer my obeisance to You," "O Shiv ji, I do Namaste to You." However, if we were to say the same thing in another language, would God not listen? Would He say that He only knows Sanskrit and that He cannot understand the simple words of another language? Definitely not! God is the knower of the hearts. If we do not utter even a single word, but simply think of Him, God will understand and reciprocate our sentiments.

So there is no need of receiving a *mantra* in the ear. God has unlimited Divine Names, and He is seated in all of them. So we can chant any of His Names, such as: Krishna, Govind, Damodar, Gopal, Ram, Shiv, Narayan, etc.

Even if the Guru gives the disciple a *mantra* in the ear, keeping it secret serves no purpose. Jagadguru Ramanujacharya's guru, Yadav Prakash, gave him a Guru *mantra*, and said, "This will be very beneficial for you. But do not reveal it to anyone." Ramanujacharya went to the crossroads, and began shouting out the *mantra* before the crowd. Yadav Prakash was informed of this by his other disciples. He called Ramanujacharya and asked him why he was disrespecting the Guru *mantra* by announcing it to the world. Ramanujacharya replied, "If it is beneficial, then why keep it secret. Let others also know it and benefit from it."

- *Swamiji*

## The Gurus of Eternally Liberated Personalities

**Question:** I have heard that Jagadguru Shree Kripaluji Maharaj does not have any Guru. Then how did he get knowledge of the scriptures?

- *Manisha Agarwal, New Brunswick, New Jersey*

**Answer:** Dear Manisha, Those who are under the bondage of Maya need a Guru to dispel their ignorance. But there are a few rare exceptional personalities, who are eternally liberated souls. They have come from the Divine Abode of God for the welfare of humankind. Such liberated souls do not have even a trace of ignorance in them. Thus, they do not need a Guru. However, for the sake of *lok ādarśh* (setting an example to humankind), they may still accept someone as their Guru.

In history, there have been two kinds of eternally liberated Saints who came to this world: those who accepted a Guru in acting, for establishing an example before the world, and those who did not make any Guru, but still possessed absolute Divine knowledge. Jagadguru Shree Kripaluji Maharaj is a Saint in the second category.

- *Swamiji*

## The *Sampradāya* of the Guru

**Question:** To which *sampradāya* (religious tradition) does Jagadguru Shree Kripaluji Maharaj belong?

- *Niranjan Satapathy, Bhanjanagar, Orissa*

**Answer:** Dear Niranjan, There are many *sampradāyas* in existence in India. Amongst the *Vaiṣhṇav sampradāyas*, four are prominent:

1. Brahma *sampradāya*, beginning from the creator Brahma. Madhvacharya and Chaitanya Mahaprabhu were the well-known *āchāryas* in this *sampradāya*.
2. Rudra *sampradāya*, beginning from God Shiv. Vishnuswami and Vallabhacharya were the important Saints in this tradition.
3. Shree *sampradāya*, beginning from Goddess Lakshmi. Ramanujacharya and Yamunacharya were the prominent Saints to appear in this *sampradāya*.
4. Kumar *sampradāya*, beginning from Sanat Kumar. Nimbarkacharya was the important Guru in this tradition.
5. Among the *non-Vaiṣhṇav sampradāyas*, the most well-known is the *sampradāya* of Shankaracharya.

Kripaluji Maharaj has preferred not to club himself in any *sampradāya*. He feels that devotees of the same one God unnecessarily divide themselves into innumerable *sampradāyas*, and then harbor ill-will towards other devotees. He explains that all the four *sampradāyas* have the same source.

For example, the Guru tradition of the Brahma *sampradāya* in reverse sequence from Madhvacharya is: Madhvacharya, Ved Vyas, Parashar, Shakti, Vasishth, Brahma, and Narayan.

The Guru tradition of the Shree *sampradāya* in reverse sequence from Ramanujacharya is: Ramanujacharya, Yamunacharya, Ram Mishra, Pundarikaksha, Nath Muni, Shathkop, Parshad, Vishvaksena, Laxmi, and Narayan.

The Guru tradition of Shankaracharya's *sampradāya* in reverse sequence is: Shankaracharya, Govindacharya, Gaudapadacharya, Shukadev Paramahans, Ved Vyas, Parashar, Shakti, Vasishth, Brahma, and Narayan.

We see that each of these *sampradāyas* has begun from the Supreme Lord Narayan. When they all have one source, why divide them into four, based on an intermediate *āchārya*? And if we do so, the parts will get further divided into more segments with subsequent *āchāryas*.

That is exactly what has happened. In the Brahma *sampradāya*, there are eight segments that exist in the main center of Udipi. Apart from these is the Gaudiya branch of the same *sampradāya* that is especially prominent in West Bengal. This is divided into Prācheen Gaudiyas and Naveen Gaudiyas. The Naveen Gaudiyas are divided into Gaudiya Math and ISKCON. The same innumerable divisions exist in the other *sampradāyas* as well.

Seeing the prevailing scenario, Jagadguru Shree Kripaluji Maharaj preferred not to limit himself to any one *sampradāya*. That is also probably the reason why he has not accepted anyone as his Guru, so as to prevent being branded in any of the *sampradāyas*. He explains that there are only two *sampradāyas*: one is the *sampradāya* of God and the other is the *sampradāya* of Maya. There is no need for any further partitions.

- *Swamiji*

16

# Meditation and *Sādhanā*

## Fluctuations of the mind

**Question:** Why do our feelings of love for God and Guru vary throughout the day? At times, they are very strong and for a large part of the day or night, there is no feeling at all. There are many occasions when a *sādhak* has negative thoughts or feelings towards God. Why does this happen? How does one stop it?

- *Meena Shrivastav, Lucknow, Uttar Pradesh*

**Answer:** Dear Meena, Our devotional feelings vary throughout the day because of the presence of the three *guṇas* in the mind. This has been explained in detail in the chapter titled "How to Deal with the World." The material energy, Maya, has three modes, or *guṇas*—*sattva guṇa*, *rajo guṇa*, and *tamo guṇa*. The mind is made from Maya, and it too contains these three *guṇas*. As these *guṇas* vary throughout the day, a person's thoughts too keep fluctuating.

To give an example, when *sattva guṇa* becomes prominent in the mind, you may start thinking, "I have received so much Grace from my Guru. The human form is precious and it should not be wasted in mundane pursuits, so I should endeavor to progress rapidly in my *sādhanā*." When *rajo guṇa* becomes prominent, you may think, "I must surely progress on the spiritual path, but what is the hurry?

At present, I have many responsibilities to discharge, and they are more important." When *tamo guṇa* dominates, you could think, "I am not really sure if there is any God or not, for no one has ever seen Him. So why waste time in *sādhanā*?" Notice how the same person's thoughts have oscillated from such heights to the depths of devotion.

For the mind to fluctuate due to the three *guṇas* is very natural. If it remained at the highest consciousness all day, there would be no need for *sādhanā*. *Sādhanā* means to fight with the flow of the three *guṇas* in the mind, and force it to maintain devotional feelings towards God and Guru. Though the mind's natural sentiments may be inclined towards the world, yet with the intellect, we force it into the spiritual realm. Initially, this may seem difficult, but with practice it will become easy. This is just as driving a car is difficult in the beginning, but with practice it becomes natural.

The problem in this process is that we do not see the mind as different from ourselves. And so when the mind presents a disturbing thought, we feel, "Oh! I am thinking in this negative manner." We begin to associate with the poisonous thought, allow it to reside in us, and damage us spiritually. To the extent that even if the mind presents a thought against God and Guru, we accept the thought as ours. If, at that time, we could see the mind as separate from ourselves, we would be able to dissociate from that negative thought. We could then chastise the mind, "I will have nothing to do with any thought that is not conducive to my devotion."

Jagadguru Shree Kripaluji Maharaj says:

मन को मानो शत्रु उसकी, सुनहु जनि कछु प्यारे।

*mana ko māno śhatru usakī, sunahu jani kachhu pyāre*

*(Sādhanā Karu Pyāre)*

"Declare war on your mind. Do the opposite of what it says, and soon it will stop bothering you."

Jagadguru Shankaracharya also stated:

जगद् जितं केन? मनो ही येन।।

*jagad jitaṁ kena? mano hī yena*

"Who will conquer the world? One who conquers the mind." Saint Tulsidas ji has repeatedly and severely chastised his mind in his *bhajans* in the "Vinay Patrikā."

So do not be disappointed if the mind troubles you and repeatedly runs to the world. Put on the spiritual armor (*tattvagyān*) given by your Gurudev, and begin the fight.

- *Swamiji*

## The Benefits of Meditation

**Question:** Dear Swamiji, I am eagerly looking forward to reading your book. Please accept a question from my side as well. What are the benefits of meditation?

- *Shyama Devi Dasi, Los Angeles, California*

**Answer:** Dear Shyama Devi, Meditation is a means of elevating the mind to Divine consciousness, for reaching the ultimate goal of life, which is Divine Love for God.

All day long people work and live in a material environment that pulls their minds towards the world. Meditation fills the mind with devotion, detaches it from the world, attaches it on God, and results in the purification of consciousness. This surcharging of consciousness through meditation benefits one throughout the day.

Consider the analogy of milk. If you pour water in it, the milk is unable to remain separate from it and retain its pure identity. However, if you keep the water separate from the milk and convert it into yogurt, and then extract butter from the yogurt, that butter can then challenge the water, "Mr. Water! I will sit on your head and float. You cannot do anything to me. As long as I was milk, you would mix within me and dilute my concentration. But now, I have become butter, and thus I am immiscible."

Similarly, in isolation from the disturbing elements of the world, if we learn to focus our mind on God for some time, it will help us in sustaining Divine consciousness throughout the day, even while working in the world. Like the sandalwood tree, we too will live in the world but not let the world live within us.

चन्दन विष व्यापै नहीं, लिपटे रहत भुजँग।

*chandana viṣha vyāpai nahīñ, lipaṭe rahata bhujaṅga*

"Although the sandalwood tree has venomous cobras lying encircled around it, their poison does not affect the tree."

Meditation has innumerable other benefits too. Modern scientists estimate that we use only three percent of the mind's potential. The reason for this is that our mind is scattered, and it keeps flitting from topic to topic and thought to thought. But if we can learn to concentrate our mind, we can increase the utilization of our mental and intellectual faculties.

Meditation also has a very salubrious effect on physical health. Most ailments have their roots in the mind. When one harbors poisonous thoughts, of hatred, envy, anxiety, tension, fear, etc., it disturbs the mental sheath (one of the five sheaths in the body). This disturbance is then passed on to the *prāṇic* sheath, which then manifests in the physical sheath of the body as disease. Meditation on God heals the various ailments of the mind, resulting in enhancement of vital energy and the improvement of physical health as well.

- *Swamiji*

## Proper Process of Meditation

**Question:** In New York, teaching meditation has become a business, and there are as many kinds of meditation as there are teachers. This has created a very confusing scenario for beginners like me. Can you please clear my confusion and explain what the proper process of meditation is?

- *Jaswinder Singh, Jackson Heights, New York*

**Answer:** Dear Jaswinder, Different peoples in different cultures around the world use a variety of meditational techniques to improve their concentration. Some meditate on the breath, others on the centre of the eyebrows, other on the psychic centers in the spinal column, yet others on a still lake, and still others on a light, etc. These different meditations do improve the focus of the mind, but their benefits are incomplete and impermanent. The reason is that they do not address the issue of purification of the mind. And as long as lust, anger, greed, envy, illusion, etc., reside in the mind, these forces again destroy the enhanced concentration. Thus, it becomes vitally important to understand how to purify the mind.

For cleansing the mind, we must fix it on an object of meditation that is pure. The material realm is dominated by the three modes of nature—*sattva*, *rajas*, and *tamas* (goodness, passion, and ignorance). If the object of meditation is material, it cannot purify the mind. Beyond this material realm, is the Divine realm of God—His Names, Forms, Virtues, Abodes, Pastimes, and Saints. If we fix our mind anywhere in this area, it will become pure. Shree Krishna instructed Arjun:

मां च योऽव्यभिचारेण भक्तियोगेन सेवते।
स गुणान्समतीत्यैतान्ब्रह्मभूयाय कल्पते।। (गीता १४.२६)

*mām cha yo 'vyabhichāreṇa bhaktiyogena sevate*
*sa guṇānsamatītyaitānbrahmabhūyāya kalpate*
*(Bhagavad Geeta 14.26)*

"I am Divine. If you fix your mind on Me, it will rise above the three modes of Maya."

Jagadguru Shankaracharya said:

शुद्धयति हि नान्तरात्मा कृष्णपदाम्भोज भक्तिमृते।।

*śhuddhayati hi nāntarātmā kṛiṣhṇapadāmbhoja bhaktimṛite*

"The inner self, the mind, cannot be cleansed without fixing it in devotion of God."

If we see the scenario around us, we find people meditating upon *chakras*, the breath, the tip of the nose, the center of the eyebrows, and so on. But very few people even have the knowledge that they are supposed to meditate upon God. One technique has been given the name "Transcendental Meditation", but the object of meditation is not transcendental. True transcendental meditation is that where we meditate upon the Lord, Who is transcendental to the material realm.

Jagadguru Shree Kripalu ji Maharaj says:

सर्व शास्त्र सार यह गोविन्द राधे।
आठों याम मन हरि गुरु में लगा दे।। (राधा गोविन्द गीत)

*sarva śhāstra sāra yaha govinda rādhe*
*āṭhoñ yāma mana hari guru meñ lagā de (Rādhā Govinda Gīta)*

"The essence of all the scriptures is to always attach the mind to God and Guru." Hence in Jagadguru Kripaluji Yog, we learn to meditate on the Names, Forms, Virtues, Pastimes, Abodes, and Associates of God.

Thus, to answer your question in one sentence: The proper technique of meditation is to focus the mind upon God. (The process for doing this will be explained in the answer to the next question.)

- *Swamiji*

## *Roop Dhyān*—Meditation on the Form of God

**Question:** The goal of meditation is to still the mind, but this seems impossible to me. My mind wanders aimlessly when I sit to meditate, and I feel dejected by this. How can I still my restless mind? Kindly enlighten.

- *Carlos Barito, Pearland, Texas*

**Answer:** Dear Carlos, The mind is such a machine created by God that it cannot remain empty; it keeps working on something or the other. To still the mind into a state of thoughtlessness creates an unstable condition for the mind that is difficult to maintain. This is just as while riding a bicycle, if you apply the brakes and bring the bicycle to a standstill, you will fall either to the left or to the right. But if you simply turn the handle to one side, the cycle will stop moving forward and very easily turn in the direction of the handle.

Meditational techniques for stopping the thought process and stilling the mind are highly unsuccessful. In *Bhakti Yog*, we do not try to still the mind; we divert it to God. Please read the answer to the previous question, to get a detailed explanation of this. Now, I would like to explain to you how to meditate upon God.

In endless past lifetimes we have been habituated to interacting with forms. All the personalities we loved and all the objects we were attached to had forms, and so attraction to forms is a natural *sanskār* (tendency) of the mind. So make the Form of God as the basis of your meditation. If we endeavor to meditate merely upon the Name of God, or the syllable "Om", the mind will not easily experience sweetness in it. But if we have the all-attractive form of God before us, the mind will effortlessly be drawn towards it. This meditation upon the form of God is called *Roop Dhyān*. Jagadguru Shree Kripaluji Maharaj states:

सब साधन जनु देह सम, रूप ध्यान जनु प्रान।
खात गीध अरु स्वान जनु, कामादिक शव मान।।

*saba sādhana janu deha sama, rūpa dhyāna janu prāna*
*khāta gīdha aru svāna janu, kāmādika śhava māna*

*(Bhakti Śhatak 10)*

"All spiritual practices are like the body; meditation upon the form of God is like the life airs. Just as the body without life airs is worthy of being eaten by dogs and vultures, similarly *sādhanā* without meditation upon the form of God, is eaten by lust, anger, greed, and envy."

- *Swamiji*

## Meditating on Material Form for Divine Results

**Question:** You ask us to make the form of God with the mind. But that is only a material form, so how can it give the Divine results that a meditator seeks?

- *Hrima Dixit, Bridgewater, New Jersey*

**Answer:** Dear Hrima, Often those who meditate upon a formless light believe they are engaging in transcendental meditation, and think that meditation on God's personal form is a material meditation. However, the Ramayan states:

गो गोचर जहँ लगि मन जाई। सो सब माया जानेहु भाई।।

*go gochara jahañ lagi mana jāī, so saba māyā jānehu bhāī*

*(Ramayan)*

"The mind is made from Maya, and wherever it can reach is the realm of Maya." If you meditate upon the form of God, it is merely a conception of the material mind; it is not the Divine form of God. Also, if you meditate on the formless *Brahm*, again it is merely a light created by your mind; it is not the Divine light of God. Hence, transcendental meditation by the material mind is not possible, be it on the formless or on the personal form of God.

Meditation upon the Divine is only achievable when God bestows His Grace and makes the mind Divine, by His *Yogmāyā* power. Until then, we have to continue with the material meditation. But we can create Divine sentiments towards the object of our meditation, and those sentiments will purify the mind.

So do not worry that the form of God you are making with your mind is material. Use that form to increase your love for Him, by developing Divine sentiments towards Him. When you reach the state of मामेकं शरणं व्रज। *māmekaṁ śharaṇaṁ vraja*, "Complete surrender to God," He will bestow His Grace upon you and make your mind Divine. Then you will not need to create a form of God with your mind. You will see Him as He is, standing before you, in His actual Divine form.

Therefore, in the meditation that you do at present, there is no stipulated form that you must focus upon. You can choose any form of God that you are attracted to, or create His form with your mind; but keep Divine sentiments to increase your love for Him.

- *Swamiji*

## Meditating on Material Personalities

**Question:** Swamiji I have a query regarding the form of the Lord in *Roop Dhyān*. Since my childhood whenever I imagine about Lord Krishna, the form of the Lord that I saw on the TV serial Mahabharat comes to my mind. When I see Mahabharat's Lord Krishna I feel as if He is my Beloved Lord Himself and not any character played by the actor. But all my friends and relatives warn me that I am doing a sin worshiping an actor in the costume of Lord Krishna. Please help me, Swamiji. Shall I meditate on the Lord's form as portrayed by the actor? Or is it a sin as thought of by my relatives?

- *Sonali Gupta, Greater Kailash, Delhi*

**Answer:** Dear Sonali, For *Roop Dhyān*, the form of God that you meditate upon can either be made by the mind, according to your liking, or you can take the help of a deity or picture of God, and meditate upon it. Now your question is that instead of the deity etc., you wish to meditate upon the form of an actor who played the role of Shree Krishna in the famous Mahabharat TV serial.

This is not wrong. If you attach the mind to that form with the sentiments that this is the Supreme Lord Shree Krishna, you will get the benefit of your sentiments. This is like when one worships a stone deity with sentiments that it is Lord Krishna, one gets the benefit of engaging in devotion to God. The Lord is seated in your heart and notes and rewards the Divine sentiments. Similarly, if you worship the form of a TV actor with the sentiments that it is the Supreme Lord, you will get Divine results.

However, it is usually not recommended that you meditate upon a living material personality. Tomorrow if you hear about his faults, you will not be able to retain your Divine sentiments. Hence it is suggested that either you imagine the form of God with your mind itself, or else take the support of a deity or a picture, where there is no scope for seeing faults.

*- Swamiji*

## *Brahm Muhūrt*

**Question:** I am told it is best to wake up by "*Brahm muhūrt*" and remember God. What is *Brahm muhūrt*?

*- Neelmani Yadav, Rohtak, Haryana*

**Answer:** Dear Neelmani, Technically, *Brahm muhūrt* is two hours before sunrise until sunrise. However, since the sunrise time in the higher latitudes varies tremendously from summer to winter, *Brahm muhūrt* could be taken to mean the two early morning hours before breakfast.

*Brahm muhūrt* is the best time for *sādhanā* because, having just woken up from sleep, your mind is empty in the morning, and it can easily be fixed on God. But as you go through your daily activities, the mind starts filling up with the impressions and thoughts of the world, making it more difficult to fix it upon God.

Besides, in the early morning hours the environment is tranquil, the atmosphere is less polluted and disturbing sounds are fewer. For all these reasons, the early morning *Brahm muhūrt* hours are considered best for *sādhanā*.

*- Swamiji*

## The Duration of Meditation

**Question:** I have another question. How long should we meditate?

*- Neelmani Yadav, Rohtak, Haryana*

**Answer:** Dear Neelmani, Ideally, the rule is that we should give back to God one-tenth of what we get. The scriptures instruct us to give away one-tenth of our income in the service of God and Guru. In addition, we have received twenty four hours from the Lord, so we should give back one-tenth of this time to Him. Thus, it is recommended that we should spend two hours on *sādhanā*. This can either be spent entirely on meditation, or divided between the different forms of *sādhanā* that one practices.

*- Swamiji*

## The Importance of Contemplation

**Question:** In the writing of some Christian saints, emphasis is laid on contemplation. What is its place in devotional practice of the Hindu religion?

*- Damini Nedungadi, Kuala Lumpur, Malaysia*

**Answer:** Dear Damini, Contemplation is called *Chintan*, or *Manan*, in the Vedas. It means repeatedly bringing any aspect of Divine knowledge to the intellect. First, we hear the knowledge of the scriptures from the Guru; this is called *Śhravaṇ*. Then we contemplate on what we have heard or read; this is called *Chintan*.

This *Chintan* or contemplation helps to strengthen the knowledge in the intellect. It is one of the most potent means of illuminating the intellect with the light of Divine knowledge. The power of *chintan* is such that if it is misused, it becomes *chintā* (worry), and it can lead to suicide. Let us say that a student fails in his school's final examination. Hundreds of other students fail too, but this student starts contemplating, "What will I do now? How will I show my face to my parents? What will my friends say? Life is not worth living. It is useless to exist. It is better that I die." This thought process goes out of control to such an extent that the student commits suicide. His class-fellows wonder what happened that made him take such a drastic step? This was all a result of misdirected contemplation.

The same power of contemplation, if properly directed, can lead to God-realization. We could repeatedly think, "Shree Krishna alone is mine. He is so kind and merciful. He has been sitting in my heart since endless lifetimes. He is my eternal Father, Mother, Friend, and Master." Such contemplation will elevate the mind to sublime heights, enhance love for God, and boost devotional sentiments.

For example, we are naturally attracted to people's qualities, but God has unlimited qualities and yet our mind feels no attraction towards Him. This is because we have never thought deeply about them. If we repeatedly think how beautiful He is, how merciful He is, etc., our love for God will grow rapidly. Contemplation is thus an important part of the daily spiritual practice.

- *Swamiji*

## The Importance of *Kīrtans* and *Bhajans*

**Question:** Do singing *bhajans* and listening to them help us in getting closer to God in any way?

- *Harbans Kaur, Sunnyvale, CA*

**Answer:** Dear Harbans, Singing *bhajans* and *kīrtans* is a powerful way of thinking of God. If I were to ask you to sit and contemplate on Radha Krishna, you would probably be at a loss regarding what to think. But the sweet *bhajans* and *kīrtans* written by the Saints describe the Divine Names, Forms, Virtues, Pastimes, and Abodes of God. When we sing them, the mind naturally dwells upon their meaning. The *bhajans* and *kīrtans* become aids to contemplation and meditation.

Singing the glories of God is thus a very important form of devotion. This is called *kīrtan*. We then hear the glories with our ears; that is called *śhravaṇ*. And then we ponder over the subject matter with our mind; this is called *manan*. This three-fold method of *śhravaṇ*, *kīrtan*, and *smaraṇ* is the easiest form of devotional and spiritual practice. It is also the most powerful.

Hence, the Vedic scriptures have greatly extolled the virtues of kīrtan:

कलेर्दोष निधेराजन्नस्तिह्येको महान् गुणः।
कीर्तनाद् एव कृष्णस्य मुक्तसंगः परं व्रजेत्।। (श्रीमद् भागवतम्)

*kalerdoṣha nidherājannastihyeko mahān guṇaḥ*
*kīrtanād eva kṛiṣhṇasya muktasaṅgaḥ paraṁ vrajet*
*(Shreemad Bhagavatam 12.3.51)*

"*Kaliyug* is an ocean of faults, but it has one great quality. By doing *kīrtan* of Shree Krishna, one is easily liberated from Maya and attains the Divine Abode."

अविकारी वा विकारी वा सर्व दोषैक भाजनः।
परमेश परं याति रामनामाभि शंकया।। (अध्यात्म रामायण)

*avikārī vā vikārī vā sarva doṣhaika bhājanaḥ*
*parameśha paraṁ yāti rāmanāmābhi śhaṅkayā*
*(Adhyātma Rāmāyaṇ)*

"Whether one is without desires, or full of desires, faultless or full of faults, if one chants the Names of Shree Ram, one will attain God-realization."

पापानलस्व दीप्तस्य मा कुवेतु भयं नराः।
गोविन्द नाम मेघौघेर्नष्यते नीर बिन्दुभिः।। (गरुड़ पुराण)

*pāpānalasva dīptasya mā kuvetu bhayaṁ narāḥ*
*govinda nāma meghaughernaśhyate nīra bindubhiḥ*
*(Garuḍ Purāṇa)*

"Humans should not worry about the burning fire of past sins; the rain showers from the clouds of God's Holy Name will extinguish it easily."

हरेर्नाम हरेर्नाम हरेर्नामैव केवलम्।
कलौ नास्त्येव नास्त्येव नास्त्येव गतिर्न्यथा।।

*harernāma harernāma harernāmaiva kevalam*
*kalau nāstyeva nāstyeva nāstyeva gatiranyathā*

*(Bṛihan Nāradīya Purāṇa)*

"Declare it three times that the name of God is my very life. In *Kaliyug* there is no other means for salvation, no other means, no other means."

एहिं कलिकाल न साधन दूजा, जोग जज्ञ जप तप व्रत पूजा।
रामहि सुमिरिअ गाइअ रामहि, संतत सुनिअ राम गुन ग्रामहि।।

*ehiñ kalikāla na sādhana dūjā, joga jagya japa tapa vrata pūjā*
*rāmahi sumiria gāia rāmahi, santata sunia rāma guna grāmahi*

*(Ramayan)*

"In this age of *Kali* no other spiritual practice is successful, neither *Aṣhṭāṅg Yog*, fire sacrifice, chanting on the rosary, austerities, or fasts. Simply sing the glories of Ram, hear them from the Saints, and remember them in the mind."

\- *Swamiji*

# 17

# YOG

## Blending Materialism and Spirituality

**Question:** Spirituality makes us oblivious to the luxuries of the body. Materialism makes us neglect the spirit. Is it possible to blend both, spirituality and materialism, in our lives?

- *Natubhai Bhakta, Clearwater, Florida*

**Answer:** Dear Natubhai, The attainment of a healthy mind in a healthy body requires a synthesis of both—material and spiritual knowledge. No matter how successful we become in our field of work, if the body is ailing and the mind is disturbed, we will remain unhappy. Hence, our most valuable possession is not our wealth, property, or car, but our own body and mind. The body, which is made from the five material elements and sustained by what we eat and drink, must be kept in good shape through material science. And the mind must be cleansed and elevated through spiritual science. Hence, there is the need to blend both, spiritual and material sciences, in our lives.

Simplistic spiritual practitioners sometimes proclaim that since we are the soul, we must cultivate only the spirit and pay no attention to the body. However, if the body falls sick, the mind becomes filled with the sensation of physical pain, and one cannot even think of God.

A healthy body is our boat for crossing the ocean of material existence. The old adage states: "Health is wealth." Realizing the truth of this, an intelligent person should spend time and effort to learn the science of healthy living, for physical and mental well-being.

Conversely, materialists often proclaim spiritual science as a waste of time and an impediment to material progress. This is also naïve, for without the help of spiritual knowledge, secular science has no means of eliminating the negative propensities of the mind. We may harness external nature through modern technology to multiply our bodily comforts, but how will we harness the forces of our internal nature, such as lust, anger, greed, envy, and illusion? This is only possible by taking recourse to spirituality.

Thus, for attaining the Ultimate goal of human life, we need to adopt both—spirituality for nourishing the mind and materialism for taking care of the body.

*- Swamiji*

## Why *Yogāsans* Are So Effective

**Question:** The popularity of Yoga has skyrocketed around the world. What is the science behind the effectiveness of the *Yogāsans*?

*- Brenda Whitney, Ventura County, California*

**Answer:** Dear Brenda, The art of healthy living must incorporate all aspects of the personality—the physical, mental, emotional, intellectual, and spiritual. While the central theme of *Yog* remains the highest goal of the spiritual path, physical yogic practices enshrined in it, give direct and tangible benefits to everyone regardless of their spiritual aims.

*Yogāsans* harmonize the body, mind, and emotions. For example, at the physical level, organs, muscles, and nerves may not be functioning properly. *Āsans* bring the different bodily parts into perfect coordination so that they work for the good of the whole body.

At the mental level, people harbor poisonous thoughts and emotions within. Muscular knots may occur anywhere in the body—in the neck as cervical spondylitis, in the face as neuralgia, etc. Every mental knot has a corresponding physical, muscular knot, and vice versa. For example, emotional tensions can affect the smooth functioning of the lungs and the breathing process, contributing to a very debilitating disease, which is asthma. The aim of *āsans* is to release these knots.

For full benefit, these *āsans* should be performed along with meditation. Meditational exercises cleanse the mind, to bring a feeling of peace and contentment within. Proper combinations of *āsans*, *pranayam*, subtle body relaxation, and meditation, tackle these knots, both at the physical and mental levels. As a result of the release of dormant energy, the body becomes full of vitality and strength, the mind becomes light and creative, joyful and balanced.

*Yogāsans* have succeeded as an alternative therapy in diseases such as asthma, diabetes, blood pressure, arthritis, digestive disorders, and many ailments of a chronic and constitutional nature, where modern medical science has failed.

- *Swamiji*

## *Yogāsans* versus Exercises

**Question:** What is the difference between *Yogāsans* and Exercises?

- *Sirjana Shreshta, Asheville, North Carolina*

**Answer:** Dear Sirjana, Exercises impose a beneficial stress on the body. Without them, the muscles waste, the bones become weak, the capacity to absorb oxygen decreases, and the ability to meet demands of sudden physical activity is lost. However, exercises work only on the muscles. They cause catabolism, or breakdown of cells.

*Āsans* work on the organs, nerves, and glands, and alter the electro-chemical activity in the nervous system. They increase the oxygen in the blood, lower the bodily temperature, and slow down metabolic rates.

- *Swamiji*

## Static vs Dynamic *Yogāsan*

**Question:** What is the difference between static and dynamic *āsans*?

*- Sosheel Sharma, Kuala Lumpur, Malaysia*

**Answer:** Dear Sosheel, Dynamic *āsans* involve energetic movements of the body; they can include a sequence of multiple *āsans*. They are not intended to develop muscles, but to increase the flexibility of the body, speed up circulation, loosen muscles and joints, release energy blocks, and remove stagnant blood from different parts of the body. Surya Namaskar is an example of dynamic *āsans*.

Static *āsans* have a powerful effect on the subtle body and the *prāṇs*. They are performed with little or no movement. The aim is to gently massage the internal organs, glands, and muscles as well as to relax the nerves throughout the body. They are specifically concerned with bringing tranquility to the mind.

*- Swamiji*

## Proper Time for *Yogāsan*

**Question:** What is the best time for doing Yoga?

*- Stephen Zamansky, Houston, Texas*

**Answer:** Dear Stephen, The best time for practicing *Yogāsans* is *Brahm muhūrt*, or the morning hours before breakfast. At this time the activities of the stomach and the intestines have stopped, the mind has no deep impressions on the conscious level and it is empty of thoughts.

The muscles are stiffest in the morning, yet through the session of *Yogāsans*, they get flexed. In the evening, two hours around sunset are also a favorable time. However, keep in mind that the *Yogāsans* must be done at least three hours after a major meal, so that the stomach is not loaded.

*- Swamiji*

## The Importance of *Mudrās*

**Question:** What is the significance of *mudrās* in *Yog* practices?

*- John Makado, Arlington, Texas*

**Answer:** Dear John, The word *mudrā* is derived from the root word "*mud*," meaning "to be glad or to delight in." *Mudrās* are postures that bring delight to the celestial beings and also to the performers. However, the term *mudrā* also denotes "seal." The hand gestures seal the body, thus preventing dissipation of bodily energy and enhancing the feeling of joyousness. They are the means of controlling the energy in the body and are also symbolic representations of our inner state.

Persons who are even slightly sensitive to the body's vibrations or energies can easily experience a change of mood by the movements of their hands. With a slight alertness, the multifarious inner states induced by the *mudrās* become clearly noticeable. People begin to feel mentally more aware of their inner vibrations and energies. It is said that there are 108 (one hundred and eight) hand gestures, which are also popular as sacred symbols in Hinduism.

*- Swamiji*

## The Importance of *Prāṇ*

**Question:** What is *prāṇ*, and what is its role in maintaining good health?

*- Deepak Subramanium, Atlanta, Georgia*

**Answer:** Dear Deepak, *Prāṇ* is a life-giving energy which is subtler than oxygen and present everywhere. It is also one of the major elements of the body and the other bodily elements remain worthless without *prāṇ*. It is *prāṇ* that gives motion to bodily parts, and everything that happens in the body is activated by *prāṇ*. It provides us with immunity to fight various diseases. It is also *prāṇ* that gives energy to the sense organs.

Our lifestyle deeply affects the *prāṇic* forces. Our actions, sleep, diet, thoughts, sensual activity, etc., all have intense effects on our *prāṇ*. An irregular and indiscriminate lifestyle depletes the *prāṇic* energy and eventually leads to *prāṇic* blockages. This is the reason why people feel loss of energy from time to time. The depletion of *prāṇic* energy leads to various ailments in the organs and muscles. The different Pranayam practices largely contribute in the expansion of *prāṇic* energy and also in the balance of the five types of *prāṇ* in the body.

- *Swamiji*

**Question:** How does *Pranayam* benefit one?

- *Jacquiline Cornelius, Corpus Christie, Texas*

**Answer:** Dear Jacquiline, In physical terms, *Pranayam* is a systematic and organized exercise of breathing which makes the lungs stronger, improves blood circulation, and alleviates many physical and mental diseases. Through a systematic exercise of breathing, the lungs become stronger, enhancing the blood circulation throughout the body.

At a subtler level, *Pranayam* is more than a respiration technique of inhalation and exhalation. The word "*Pranayam*" has been derived from two words "*prāṇ*" and "*āyām*", which means "to expand the *prāṇic* energy." Through *Pranayam*, the level of oxygen in the body definitely increases, but along with oxygen, we also take in vital *prāṇic* energy that pervades the atmosphere.

Most people use only twenty-five percent of the lungs' capacity throughout the day, in what is called "shallow breathing." Due to this, the *prāṇic* energy level in their body remains low, resulting in the appearance of multifarious ailments, such as asthma, tuberculosis, etc. Regularly performing *Pranayam* expands the *prāṇic* energy supply to all the parts of the body, and prevents these maladies.

*Pranayam* makes us mentally healthier. One should not forget the fact that imbalances in breathing hinder the physiological functions which later become psychological. *Pranayam* is effective in treating psychic disturbances, like excitement, anxiety, fear, anger, disappointment, and lasciviousness. In addition, its daily performance also results in a good memory power.

Thus, *Pranayam* has innumerable benefits that help embellish our life with a hale and hearty body and psyche.

- *Swamiji*

## What is True Yoga?

**Question:** Many people like me, who flock to Yoga studios around the world, yearn for something more substantial than the physical exercises of Yoga to satisfy our inner yearning for spirituality, Indian style. Why does this feeling persist?

- *Pamela Munrik, Manhattan, New York*

**Answer:** Dear Pamela, The craze for Yoga has definitely spread around the globe, but invariably, in the name of "Yoga," only physical exercises are taught, and people doing them feel they have become *Yogīs*. Actually, the word "Yoga" does not exist in the Sanskrit language or in the Vedic scriptures. The proper word is "*Yog*", which means "to unite." In this context, it means to unite the individual soul with the Supreme soul.

संयोगो योग इत्युक्तो जीवात्मा परमात्मनोः। (गरुड़ पुराण)

*sanyogo yoga ityukto jīvātmā paramātmanoḥ (Garuḍ Purāṇa)*

"The union of the individual soul with God is *Yog.*" This union is achieved by elevating, purifying, and focusing the mind lovingly upon Him.

The Shreemad Bhagavatam states:

एतावान् योग आदिष्टो मच्छिष्यैः सनकादिभिः।
सर्वतो मन आकृष्य मय्यद्धावेश्यते यथा।। (श्रीमद् भागवतम्)

*etāvān yoga ādiṣhṭo, machchhiṣhyaiḥ sanakādibhiḥ*
*sarvato mana ākṛiṣhya mayyaddhāveśhyate yathā*

*(Shreemad Bhagavatam 11.13.14)*

"True *Yog* means removing the mind from all the material objects of attachment, and fixing it completely on God."

Most publications and *Yog* institutions in the modern world have not endeavored to highlight the mental and spiritual aspects of *Yog*, and in the name of "Yoga," teach sincere aspirants only physical exercises and incomplete meditational techniques. Without emphasis on the purification of the mind, the hunger of the soul remains unaddressed. Those people who have deeper spiritual *sanskārs* yearn for a genuine Divine experience. That is the reason why their inner urge to understand and experience Indian spirituality remains unfulfilled.

- *Swamiji*

## Jagadguru Kripaluji Yog

**Question:** How is the system of Jagadguru Kripaluji Yog unique from the Yoga that is taught in the hundreds of Yoga studios?

- *Ashutosh Tripathy, Minneapolis, Minnesota*

**Answer:** Dear Ashutosh, Jagadguru Kripaluji Yog blends both—material and spiritual techniques—from the eternal sciences of the Vedic scriptures. It is a complete system of *Yog*, including five Vedic disciplines for mind-management and exemplary physical health. These five disciplines are:

1. Radhey Shyam Yogasans
2. Radhey Naam Pranayam
3. Subtle Body Relaxation
4. *Roop-dhyān*, or Meditation on the Form of God
5. Science of Proper Diet

The techniques of Jagadguru Kripaluji Yog have been practiced by true *yogīs* in India for millenniums. However, in their study and practice in the Western world, the role of the mind, which is the basis of elevation and degradation of a person, is not emphasized. The scriptures state:

मन एव मनुष्याणां कारणं बन्ध मोक्षयोः। (पँचदशी)
*mana eva manuṣhyāṇāṁ kāraṇaṁ bandha mokṣhayoḥ*
*(Pañchadaśhī)*

"The mind alone is the cause of bondage and liberation." If the mind is neglected, then any science for the nourishment and evolution of the personality will be incomplete and only partially effective.

In Jagadguru Kripaluji Yog, each of its five sciences is practiced with focus on purifying and elevating the mind with the help of spiritual techniques. This gives a deep satisfaction and experience of Bliss at the level of the soul. If practiced sincerely, JKYog leads to the harmonization of the mind-body-soul, a feeling of well-being from within, and the attainment of true *Yog*, or union of the individual soul with God.

- *Swamiji*

18

# Jagadguru Shree Kripaluji Maharaj

## The Title of *Jagadguru*

**Question:** What does the title of *Jagadguru* mean? Who awards the title? Please give me some information about it.

- *Poonam Sharma, Valley Ranch, California*

**Answer:** Dear Poonam, *Jagadguru* in Hinduism could be considered similar to the Pope in Christianity. "*Jagat*" means "world" and "Guru" means "Spiritual Master." So "*Jagadguru*" literally means "Spiritual Master of the world."

Divine personalities who displayed unparalleled mastery over all Vedic scriptures, and who brought about a spiritual revolution in the minds of the people by their unique explanation of Vedic knowledge, have traditionally been conferred with the title of *Jagadguru*, or Spiritual Master of the whole world. The title has been awarded to Saints who either defeated in scriptural debate, all the great scholars of their era, or were acclaimed by scholars as possessing supreme mastery of the Vedic scriptures.

In the past 5000 years of the present age of *Kali*, five personalities have been recognized as original *Jagadgurus*:

1. Jagadguru Shankaracharya: He came to the earth planet

about 2000 years ago. He re-established the greatness of Vedic *Sanātan Dharm* in India. His philosophy is known as *Advait-vād* or Non-dualism. He established four seats, called *Maṭhs*, for the propagation of Vedic religion.

2. Jagadguru Nimbarkacharya: He appeared in the world shortly after Shankaracharya. He propounded the philosophy of *Dvait-Advait-vād* or Dualistic Non-dualism, which states that the soul and God have perfect oneness and yet perfect duality. He emphasized devotion to Radha Krishna.

3. Jagadguru Ramanujacharya: He appeared on this earth planet about 1,000 years ago. His philosophy is known as *Viśhiṣhṭ-Advait-vād*, or Qualified Non-dualism. He put great emphasis on surrender to God, and established the proper system of worship in temples throughout India.

4. Jagadguru Madhvacharya: He descended about 700 years ago, and was the vigorous propagator of *Dvait-vād* or the philosophy of Dualism. He stressed that the attainment of the personal form of God is the goal of all the souls, and that God, Maya, and the soul are always separate entities.

In the past, the title was not awarded by any formal body; rather, it was informally conferred on the Saints by the unanimous acclaim of the Vedic scholars of the times. The formal conferring by a body occurred only in the case of Jagadguru Shree Kripaluji Maharaj (please see next question).

- *Swamiji*

## The Fifth Original *Jagadguru*

**Question:** Nowadays, many saints have begun adding *Jagadguru* before their names. What is the difference between these self-styled jagadgurus and Kripaluji Maharaj?

- *Ramesh Patel, Ahmedabad, Gujarat*

**Answer:** Dear Ramesh, The four original *Jagadgurus* established their *Maṭhs*, or seats, in multiple places for the purpose of propagating their teachings. They appointed their senior disciples as the heads of each of these *Maṭhs*. These disciples also began calling themselves "jagadguru". Later, when others took their place, they too took on the title for themselves. With the passage of time, other followers of that tradition began establishing newer *Maṭhs* on their own accord and became self-styled jagadgurus. That is why we see the present phenomenon where there is a proliferation of jagadgurus. However, the original *Jagadgurus* were only four.

Kripaluji Maharaj became the fifth original *Jagadguru* after a gap of 700 years, in a historical event that happened in Kashi, the holy city of Lord Shiv, in January 1957, after he gave a profound series of lectures at the invitation of the *Kāśhī Vidvat Pariṣhat*, a body of 500 topmost Vedic scholars of India. Shree Maharajji spoke for ten days, revealing the secrets of the Hindu scriptures. He reconciled the apparent contradictions between the various scriptures, and the differences between the views of the previous *Jagadgurus*, to reveal the true path to God-realization for the welfare of all humankind, relevant to the present times.

With profound admiration, the scholars accepted that his knowledge was deeper than the combined knowledge of all 500 of them put together. They unanimously acclaimed him as *Jagadguru*, the Spiritual Master of the world. They further added that he was "***Jagadguruttam***," or Supreme amongst all *Jagadgurus*. Among the various accolades that they showered upon him, was "*Bhakti-Yog Rasāvatār*," or the personification of the Bliss of Divine Love.

- *Swamiji*

## Brief Account of Maharajji's Life

**Question:** Can you please give me some information about the life and works of Jagadguru Kripalu Maharaj, for I feel I will be inspired by it?

- *Nicolas Ivanovitch, Samara, Russia*

**Answer:** Dear Nicolas, Eternally liberated Saints sometimes descend upon the earth, from the Divine abode of God, for the welfare of humankind. Jagadguru Shree Kripaluji Maharaj is such a Divine personality. "Shree Maharajji", as he is lovingly called by his devotees, was born on the auspicious full-moon night of *Śharat Pūrṇimā*, in the month of October, in 1922, in the village Mangarh, near Allahabad in India.

He spent his childhood in youthful fun, playing games and frolicking with his young friends. But at the same time, he would display intense gravity and excel effortlessly in his studies. Then at the age of fourteen, he left the village and attended three Universities, in Kashi, Chitrakoot, and Indore. There he covered a whole series of courses in the space of just two-and-a-half years.

At the young age of sixteen, he suddenly gave up his studies and entered the dense forests of Chitrakoot. There he spent his time absorbed in intense love for Radha Krishna. Often he would lose all external consciousness, and go without eating and drinking for many days at a stretch. For long periods, he would remain in *Mahābhāv*, the highest stage of devotion that manifests in Radha Rani, the Divine Mother of the Universe. The very same manifestation of *Mahābhāv* love was last seen in Chaitanya Mahaprabhu, about 500 years ago. Maharajji emerged from the forest after two years to begin his mission of revealing the glories of the path of Divine Love to the world.

He then started conducting *satsaṅgs*, congregational spiritual programs, that brought about a *Bhakti* revolution in the states of Uttar Pradesh and Rajasthan in the 1940s and 50s. He would lead devotional chantings imbued with intense devotion, which would continue throughout the night. These *kīrtans*, which he wrote himself, have been compared by scholars with those of Meerabai, Soordas, Tulsidas, and Ras Khan. Shree Maharajji's Divine *kīrtans* have secured a place for themselves in the hearts of devotees across the globe.

After accepting the title of *Jagadguru*, Kripaluji Maharaj traveled throughout India for fourteen years. He would deliver month-long discourses in each city, unraveling the mysteries of the scriptures before tens of thousands of people who would throng his lectures. Shree Maharajji's lectures enchanted the masses with humor, worldly examples, practical instructions, and playful chastisement, much to the delight of the crowd. It was a unique experience as he made the deepest scriptural truths accessible to everyone in the simplest language.

It is Shree Maharajji's vision that every soul should get a chance to practice *Bhakti* or devotion in its simplest form, so that the soul may attain its true goal of God-realization. In order to help people around the world in their quest towards this goal, Shree Maharajji has trained devotee preachers and sent them to different parts of the globe. He has also created huge *āśhrams*, to provide facilities for devotees who wish to practically apply the teachings in their lives.

*- Swamiji*

## *Kīrtans* Written by Maharajji

**Question:** Can you please tell me about the importance and specialty of the *kīrtans* written by Shree Maharajji?

*- Poonam Sharma, Valley Ranch, California*

**Answer:** Dear Poonam, Jagadguru Shree Kripaluji Maharaj has written thousands of inspiring verses revealing the Divine pastimes of Radha Krishna. His style of writing is unique in the entire history of saints. First, he begins the chanting of a *pada* or *kīrtan*, and as the *kīrtan* progresses, he keeps adding lines to it, finally bringing it to a consummate close. In glorification of Shree Radha Krishna devotion, he has named one of his principal creations as "*Prem Ras Madirā*," or "Divine Love Intoxicant." One is lost for words to describe the intensity and greatness of the *padas* or *kīrtans* written by Shree Maharajji. It is only by singing the divinely intoxicating *kīrtans* that we can get a glimpse of the unfathomable Divine love that pours out from the heart of a true devotee of Shree Radha Krishna.

The *kīrtans* conducted by Shree Maharajji are famous for the fervent intensity of devotion that they create in the minds and hearts of the sincere follower, forever binding him or her to the path of

God-realization. Whenever Shree Maharajji graces the prayer and *Sādhanā* hall, the *kīrtans* reach a feverish pitch as the Lord's names and pastimes are sung in unison by ecstatic voices across the floor. These highly charged *kīrtans* mesmerize even the most phlegmatic of people, drawing them ever closer to Shree Radha Krishna.

*- Swamiji*

## The Divine Mother of Our Mission

**Question:** Seeing your deep devotion, surrender, and respect for Jagadguru Shree Kripaluji Maharaj has inspired me to come closer to him myself, and I look on him as a descension of Chaitanya Mahaprabhu Himself. But I am confused about the position of his wife, Amma ji, in his mission.

*- Pavitra Routray, Bhowani Patna, Odisha*

**Answer:** Dear Pavitra, Our Divine Mother, Shree Maharajji's wife, whom we devotees lovingly called "Amma," had descended to assist Shree Maharajji in his mission of distributing Divine love of Radha Krishna to evolved souls on this planet. She was born on Divali day in the year 1925, in a small village called Leelapur, about 100 kilometers from Mangarh. Her father was a great Sanskrit scholar and devotee. She was married to Maharajji in her childhood itself, in accordance with the tradition of child marriage prevalent in Uttar Pradesh at that time. In her youth, she stayed mostly in Mangarh, while Maharajji would go on preaching tours for eleven months in a year.

As the *satsaṅg* grew and thousands of *satsaṅgīs* became a part of the mission, she showered her love on them, and helped them in their devotion to Shree Maharajji. While Maharajji, as the perfect Spiritual Master, was often as hard as a thunderbolt, Amma was the soft, forgiving, patient, and caring mother, whose love could always be counted upon. While Maharajji maintained an externally strict profile, Amma provided the gentle human touch that gave so much strength to the devotees in their arduous journey to God-realization.

Amma's life was always one of sacrifice for her Divine Beloved. She never complained about having no opportunity for personal time with Maharajji. His happiness was her only consideration throughout her life, and she sacrificed her all for it. She was thus the epitome of purity, and selfless devotion to her Divine husband. Amma's causeless and oceanic love could not be described in words. While Maharajji's fame spread throughout the world, and devotees came in hordes from many countries, she expanded her heart to give a place to everyone. No wonder, in her *ārati*, she is described as "Jagadamba" or Mother of the Universe.

In Amma's soft heart, the material welfare of the devotees was as important as their spiritual upliftment. I have sweet memories of how I once fell sick with cold and fever in the *āśhram*. Amma was so concerned about my illness, as if I were her own child. On the third day of the fever, I came out of the room to join the *parikramā* around the *āśhram*. On seeing that I was not resting, Amma got so annoyed that I had to at once return to my room. Such was the love that she bestowed on each and everyone who came close to her.

Amma, ended her manifest *leelas* in the material realm, and went back to the Divine Abode of Radha Krishna on 12th March, 2009. Amma's visible pastimes are no longer manifest on the earthly plane. However, in the hearts of the devotees, she will continue to live, in loving memories of her Names, Form, Virtues, Pastimes, and Abode. When we pray to her to bestow on us true love for our Guru and God, we know that she will always be there to respond to our entreaties, as generously as she did during her lifetime.

*Her little child,*

*Swami Mukundananda*

# Glossary

## A

***Abhigya Svarāṭ***—Supremely Independent (a name for God).

***Achintya Bhedābhed Vād***—Inconceivable Simultaneous Oneness and Difference. It is the name of the philosophy propounded by Chaitanya Mahaprabhu.

***Āchārya***—Spiritual teacher who is thorough with the knowledge of the scriptures.

***Ādhyātmic tāp***—Miseries arising from one's own body and mind.

***Ādibhautik tāp***—Miseries subjected from to other living beings.

***Ādidaivik tāp***—Miseries due to the forces of nature, e.g. heat, cold, etc.

***Advait Vād***—Non-dualism. It is the name of the philosophical theory propounded by Shankaracharya.

***Agni Dev***—The celestial god of fire.

***Agyān***—Ignorance.

***Ahankār***—Pride, ego.

***Akarmī***—One who performs actions but has no attachment to the fruits of the actions, and is thus considered the non-doer.

***Ānand***—The Bliss of God.

***Anāhat Chakra***—One of the seven psychic centers along the spinal column, at the heart region.

***Antaḥ Karaṇ***—Mind.

***Aṇu***—Very small.

***Apar dharm***—The social aspect of religion, including duties towards parents, friends and relatives, society, etc.

***Ārati***—Ceremony of lights, in which a lamp is waved around the deity of God with great faith and reverence.

***Arth***—Monetary resource. Economy.

***Āsan/Yogāsan***—Yogic exercise/posture for health and well-being.

***Āśhram***—Place similar to a monastery where dedicated spiritual practitioners reside.

***Aṣhṭāṅg Yog***—The eight-fold process of *Yog* described by Sage Patanjali.

***Asmitā***—Pride, ego.

***Ātmā***—The real self, or "soul," which is spiritual in nature and imparts consciousness to the body.

***Ātman***—Same as *Ātmā*.

***Avatar***—The descension of God in His personal form, in the material plane.

## B

***Bhagavad Geeta***—A popular Vedic scripture. It contains the dialogue between Shree Krishna and Arjun in 700 verses, on the battlefield of Kurukshetra.

***Bhagavad Prāpti***—God-realization.

***Bhāgavat Saptāh***—A week-long series of lectures on the Shreemad Bhagavatam.

***Bhagavān***—The Supreme Lord. The word also is used to refer to His personal form, distinct from His other aspects.

***Bhajan***—Devotional song.

***Bhakti***—Devotion.

***Bhakti Śhatak***—One hundred verses on devotion composed by Jagadguru Shree Kripaluji Maharaj.

***Bhakti Yog***—The path of attaining God through Bhakti.

***Bhaktiyog Rasāvatār***—Descension of the Bliss of Divine Love (title conferred on Jagadguru Kripaluji Maharaj by the *Kāśhī Vidvat Pariṣhat.*)

***Bharatvarsh***—The land of Bharat, the original name for India in the scriptures.

***Bhāv***—Devotional sentiment.

***Brahm***—The formless, all-pervading aspect of God.

***Brahm Gyānī***—One situated in knowledge of the formless aspect of God.

***Brahman***—The formless aspect of God, which is without Names, Virtues, and Activities.

***Brahm Muhūrt***—The two early morning hours just before sunset.

***Brahm Niṣhṭh***—One who is situated on the platform of God-realization.

***Brahmānand***—The Bliss of the formless, all-pervading aspect of God.

***Brahma***—The first created being in the material universe. Brahma, who is himself born from Lord Vishnu, creates the various life forms and the substance of the world from the material energy.

***Braj***—The land in the district of Mathura, India, where Shree Krishna performed His childhood pastimes 5000 years ago. It includes many holy places like Vrindaban, Goverdhan, Barsana, Nandagaon, and Gokul.

***Buddhi***—Intellect.

## C

***Chakra***—Psychic energy center along the channel of the spine.

***Chintā***—Worry.

***Chintan***—Repeated contemplation on something.

***Chit***—Sentient, possessing knowledge.

***Chitta***—The portion of the mind that gets attached to objects and persons.

# D

***Darśhan***—Philosophic text written by a sage.

***Deśh***—Place.

***Devatā***—Celestial god who governs some particular affairs of the material world from the higher abodes.

***Dhammapad***—The most well-known Buddhist scripture. It is a part of the Suttupitaka canon.

***Dharm***—The set of duties described by the scriptures, which are a part of religious behavior.

***Dīkṣhā***—Giving of the Divine power by the Guru to the disciple that results in God-realization. Commonly misinterpreted as receiving *mantra* in ear from guru.

***Durgā Saptaśhati***—Popular set of prayers recited to Mother Durga.

***Dvait Vād***—Dualism. It is the name of the philosophic system propounded by Madhvacharya.

***Dvait Advait Vād***—Dual-Nondualism. It is the name of the philosophic system propounded by Nimbarkacharya.

# G

***Golok***—The Divine abode of Shree Krishna, which exists in the spiritual realm, beyond this material world.

***Gopīs***—The village maidens who resided in Braj, when Shree Krishna displayed His *leelas* there 5000 years ago.

***Guru***—A God-realized teacher of spirituality who illumines people with the knowledge of God.

***Gyān***—Knowledge.

***Gyān Yog***—The path of knowing the "self" through the practice of knowledge.

***Gyānī***—One who follows the path of *Gyān Yog*.

## H

***Haṭha Yog***—A system of *sādhanā* based on physical practice and the force of will power, for preparing the body and mind for meditation.

***Hlādinī Śhakti***—The Bliss-giving power of God.

## I

***Iṣhṭa Dev***—The form of God chosen by the devotee for his or her personal devotion.

## J

***Jagadamba***—Mother of the Universe.

***Jagadguru***—Spiritual Master of the world. Equivalent to the Pope in Christianity.

***Ji***—Suffix added after someone's name as a mark of respect.

***Jīva Śhakti***—A power of God of which all the souls are tiny fragments.

## K

***Kaliyug***—The present era on the earth planet. This was preceded by *Dwāpar yug*, *Tretā yug*, and *Sat yug*.

***Kāl***—Time, as an entity that continuously flows.

***Kām***—Worldly desire. Lust.

***Karm***—Work in accordance with the prescribed rules of the Vedas.

***Karmaphal***—The fruits of past karmas that one has to bear in the present.

***Karm Yog***—The path of attaining God while doing one's *Karm*.

***Karma***—Action performed by an individual, of which God keeps an account.

***Kāśhī Vidvat Pariṣhat***—The supreme body of Vedic scholars in the city of Kashi (highest seat of Vedic learning).

***Kauravas*** —Sons of King Dhritarashtra, headed by Duryodhan.

***Khaṇḍan-Maṇḍan Paddhati***—System of presentation in which a doubt is first created amongst listeners and then resolved.

***Kīrtan***—The singing of the Names, Virtues, and Pastimes of God, usually in a group.

***Kriyamāṇ***—The karmas one performs in the present by exercise of one's free will.

***Kuber***—The celestial god of wealth.

***Kuṇḍalinī***—A power that resides at the base of the spine, like a coiled serpent. When it begins rising up the spinal column, it bestows various material mystic abilities.

## L

***Leela***—A Divine pastime enacted by God in His personal form.

***Leelapur***—A small village in Uttar Pradesh that Shreemati Padma Devi (Amma ji) chose for taking birth on earth.

***Lok Ādarśh***—Behavior or code of conduct that serves as an ideal for society to emulate.

## M

***Mādanākhya Mahābhav***—The highest level of devotion. It resides only in Radha Rani, not even in Shree Krishna.

***Madhyamākār***—Medium sized; neither infinitesimal nor infinite.

***Mahabharat***—A 100,000 verse-long poem written by Ved Vyas, describing the history of India in *Dvāpar Yug*, with emphasis on the pastimes of Shree Krishna.

***Mahābhāv***—The level of devotion that manifested in the *gopīs* of Braj.

***Mahāpralay***—The dissolution of the world at the end of creation, when it unwinds into the primordial material energy, Maya.

***Mahārājji***—It is an appellation often given to great saints. Devotees lovingly call Jagadguru Shree Kripaluji Maharaj by this name.

***Mahārās***—The Divine dance performed by Shree Krishna with the *gopīs*, filled with the Bliss of Divine Love.

***Mangarh***—The holy land in UP, forty miles from Allahabad, which was chosen by Jagadguru Shree Kripaluji Maharaj as his birthplace in the earth plane.

***Manan***—Contemplation. Repeated pondering over a truth.

***Mantra***—Sacred hymn written in Sanskrit.

***Maṭh***—The headquarters of a religious sect or denomination.

***Maya***—The material energy from which this world is created. It also puts souls, who are forgetful of God, into illusion, and makes them transmigrate in the cycle of life and death.

***Mithyā***—Non-existent, an illusion that exists only in the mind and has no objective reality.

***Mokṣh***—Liberation from the bonds of Maya.

***Mudrā***—Postures of the hand that seal and control the energy of the body.

## N

***Navarātras***—A festival of nine nights, dedicated to the worship of Mother Durga.

***Neem***—A sacred tree in India. Has bitter leaves, but highly effective medicinal properties.

***Nirguṇ***—Without qualities and form.

***Nitya Siddha Mahāpuruśh***—Eternally liberated Saint.

***Indra Dev***—The king of heaven, who is the celestial god of rain.

***Nirāśhā***—Disappointment, despair about achieving the goal.

## P

***Pada (Bhajan)***—Devotional song.

***Pāṇḍavs***—The five sons of King Pandu. Descriptions of their exploits form a major portion of the Mahabharat.

***Par Dharm***—The spiritual aspect of religion, i.e. devotion towards God.

***Parkīya Bhāv***—Devotional sentiment in which one loves God as His paramour.

***Parikramā***—Circumambulation of a sacred object as a mark of respect.

***Pātra***—Vessel.

***Prārabdh***—The destiny one is allotted at the time of birth, based on past karmas.

***Prāṇ/Prāṇic***—Life-giving energy that is subtler than air, and present everywhere.

***Pranayam***—Breathing exercise for controlling the breath and assimilating *prāṇic* energy.

***Premānand***—The Bliss of *Bhagavān*, the personal form of God.

***Prem Ras Siddhānt***—The main philosophic book written by Jagadguru Shree Kripaluji Maharaj, which summarizes the knowledge of all the Vedic scriptures and presents in a systematic and logical sequence, the simple straightforward path to God-realization for the present age.

***Prem Ras Madirā***—Set of 1008 *padas* written by Jagadguru Shree Kripaluji Maharaj, containing the treasure of Divine love for Radha Krishna.

***Premā Śhakti***—The Divine Love power of God.

***Purāṇas***—These are scriptures, full of philosophic knowledge, that discuss the creation of the universe, its annihilation and recreation, the history of humankind. There are eighteen *Puraṇas*, all written by Ved Vyas.

***Puruśhārth***—The self-effort one does in the present with the exercise of one's free will, as distinct from destiny.

***Puruśhārth Śhiromaṇi***—The highest goal worthy of striving for.

# R

***Rajo guṇa***—The mode of passion; one of the three modes of material nature.

***Rājasic***—Having the quality of *rajo guṇa*.

***Rāj Yog***—The king of *Yog*, which is devotion. *Haṭha Yogīs* like to call their practice by this name.

***Ramayan***—The historical description of the pastimes of Lord Ram in *Tretā Yug*, originally written by Sage Valmiki.

***Rās***—The Divine dance of Shree Krishna with the *gopīs* in Braj, in which He bestowed the highest Bliss of Divine love.

***Rasik***—A Saint who relishes the sweetness of devotion to Radha Krishna, in contrast to the almightiness of God.

***Roop Dhyān***—Meditation upon the Form of God.

# S

***Sādhanā***—Spiritual practice.

***Sādhan Bhakti***—Preparatory devotion, which is done to cleanse the heart and prepare it for receiving *Siddha Bhakti*.

***Sadguru***—A God-realized teacher, seated in the Truth.

***Sampradāya***—Religious tradition. Sect of devotees.

***Sanskār***—Tendencies in a person continuing from past lives.

***Sanātan Dharm***—Eternal religion. This is the name of the religion described in the Vedas. The word Hinduism was coined much later.

***Sañchit Karma***—All the accumulated karmas of the soul in endless past lifetimes.

***Sanyās***—The renounced order of life.

***Sanyāsī***—A person in the renounced order.

***Sat***—That which is eternal.

***Sattva guṇa***—The mode of goodness; one of the three modes of material nature.

***Sāttvic***—Having the quality of *sattva guṇa.*

***Sevā***—To serve, the act of service.

***Śhakti***—Energy or power.

***Sharat Pūrṇimā***—The full-moon night (usually falling on Sept/ Oct) in which Shree Krishna did the *Rās* dance.

***Śhāstras***—Scriptures.

***Śhravaṇ***—To hear spiritual knowledge.

***Shreemad Bhagavatam***—The most important of the eighteen *Purāṇas* written by Ved Vyas. It consists of 18,000 verses, full of philosophical knowledge and the descriptions of the Names, Forms, Virtues, and Pastimes of the various Avatars of God.

***Śhrotriya***—A person who is well-versed in the theoretical knowledge of the scriptures.

***Satsaṅg***—A congregation in which the Names, Virtues, and Pastimes of God are sung and remembered.

***Siddha Bhakti***—Divine Love, or perfect devotion, which is a power of God and is received by His Grace.

***Siddhis***—Material mystic abilities arising from yogic practices.

***Smaraṇ***—Remembrance of God or some spiritual truth.

***Som Ras***—Ambrosia drunk by the celestial gods.

***Sūtra***—Aphorism.

***Svānśh***—Expansions of Shree Krishna, Who are non-different from Him.

***Swarg***—The higher abodes within the material world, which have far greater facility for enjoyment than the earth planet, but are not beyond the cycle of life and death.

# T

***Tamo guṇa***—The mode of ignorance, one of the three modes of material nature.

***Tantra***—A system of spiritual practices in Hinduism and Buddhism involving sexual activity etc. for release of energy.

***Tattvagyān***—Scriptural knowledge.

# U

***Upanishads***—These are philosophical texts that constitute a section of the Vedas.

***Upāsanā***—Devotion.

# V

***Vaikunth***—The Divine abode of Lord Vishnu in the spiritual realm, beyond the material world.

***Vairāgya***—Detachment from the world.

***Varṇāśhram***—The social system, in which one's duties were defined according to one's occupation and stage in life.

***Varuṇ Dev***—The celestial god of the ocean.

***Vāsanā***—Desire.

***Vāyu Dev***—The celestial god of the wind.

***Vedas***—The eternal knowledge of God that He manifested at the beginning of creation, which was passed down from master to disciple through hearing, and finally divided and written in four books—*Ṛig* Ved, *Yajur* Ved, *Sām* Ved, and *Atharva* Ved.

***Vibhinnānśha***—Differentiated parts of God. These are the souls.

***Vibhu***—Very large.

***Viśheṣhaṇ***—Adjective that describes the quality, form, color, etc. of a noun.

***Viśhīṣhṭha Advait Vād***—Qualified Non-dualism. It is the name of the philosophy established by Jagadguru Ramanujacharya.

***Viśhuddha Advait Vād***—Pure Non-dualism. It is the name of the philosophy propounded by Vallabhacharya.

## Y

***Yantra***—Talisman. Object believed to give magical powers to one who possesses or worships it.

***Yogamāyā***—The Divine spiritual power of God.

***Yogāsan***—Yogic exercise/posture for health and well-being.

***Yogī***—One who practices *Yog*.

# Other Publications by Jagadguru Kripaluji Yog

1. Yoga for the Body, Mind, and Soul
2. Essence of Hinduism
3. Inspiring stories for Children Volume 1
4. Inspiring Stories for Children Volume 2
5. Inspiring Stories for Children Volume 3
6. Inspiring Stories for Children Volume 4
7. Saints of India
8. Festivals of India
9. Healthy Body Healthy Mind – Yoga for Children
10. Bal-Mukund Wisdom Book
11. Bal-Mukund Painting Book